FAST-STARTING A CAREER OF CONSEQUENCE

WISHING YOU A CAREER OF
CONSEQUENCE AND MANY BLESSINGS

FAST-STARTING A CAREER OF CONSEQUENCE

A lifetime of stellar leadership in business and nonprofit organizations compressed in readable and easily digestible lessons. A book of savvy coaching and spiritual advice alike! I will definitely give a copy to my son, who just graduated from college.

—Miroslav Volf
Henry B. Wright Professor of Theology,
Yale University Divinity School
Founder and Director, Yale Center for Faith and Culture

Fred Sievert brings a wealth of practical experience and a deeply embedded faith perspective to his advice about charting and pursuing a career path. This book will help those who are just beginning their career trajectory or anyone thinking about how to find a better sense of calling, vocation, and meaning in their work life.

—Brian Stogner, PhD
President, Rochester University

Work is one of our greatest blessings, and with this insightful and meaningful work, Fred Sievert unlocks specific ways that your faith in God can lift your career, enrich interactions with others, and transform every aspect of your career journey. A special self-assessment tool helps reveal what you can do to serve others in the spirit of the Gospel's teachings. A seasoned executive, theologian, and volunteer, Fred Sievert shares insights that help you chart a meaningful work/faith landscape.

—Larry Barton, PhD
Corporate Consultant
CNN and BBC Commentator on Workplace Issues

Given the plethora of self-help books available today, it's difficult to effect a separation from all the others, yet that is exactly what the author has done with *Fast-Starting a Career of Consequence*. This milestone work succeeds in combining a definitive road map for anyone entering the workforce, changing course therein, or re-entering it, with a faith-based approach founded on the very words of Jesus Christ and the Bible. Christ's teaching served as the underpinning for this work based on the experiences of a former Fortune 100 company president, Fred Sievert. In retirement, he transitioned to an enriching life serving others using a faith-based formula for life and success. Do something wonderful for yourself, and drink often from this book! It is an action plan for living significantly and successfully.

—**Phillip C. Richards, CLU®, RHU®**
Executive Chairman and Founder, North Star Resource Group
Vice Chairman, Board of Trustees, Temple University

In his important book *Fast-Starting a Career of Consequence*, Fred Sievert has paired his considerable insight into the workplace with a compassionate concern for young professionals of faith to produce a book at once practical and encouraging. This is an excellent instance of the mentoring that young professionals are hungry for and need. I only wish Fred's book had been available when I set off on my own career journey.

—**Scott G. Stephenson**
Chairman, President, and Chief Executive Officer
Verisk Analytics

Work matters. After all, God's intent was for Adam and Eve to work the Garden of Eden. And John 17 records Jesus praying, "I have brought you glory on earth by completing the work you gave me to do." Fred's book makes clear that faith and work can and should co-exist. Chapter 3 captures this concept especially well.

I love this book on several fronts: as a former senior business executive, I find Fred's advice to be on point, practical, and significant.

As a Christian, I value that his recommendations are fully bathed in appropriate Scripture. And, as a father and grandfather, the fact that he began this project out of love for his daughter is especially sweet.

I'm excited about the impact this book will have and expect that a great number will be bought for gifts. At least four of those will be purchased by me, as I have grandchildren on the cusp of entering the workplace.

—**J. Cliff Eason**
Retired President and CEO, Southwestern Bell Telephone
Current Board Chair, Reinsurance Group of America

When I read a book that I believe will enhance my personal, professional, and/or spiritual personas, I do so with three goals in mind: the book must inform, instruct, and inspire me to be my best self. *Fast-Starting a Career of Consequence* is such a book. It is a grand slam.

Fred humbly informs his readers on how to get the best impact from the lessons covered through sharing personal stories from his life while tying in Scriptural guidance. As a close friend would, he takes the time to inspire us to use the content for the betterment of ourselves, for the benefit of our companies, and for the good of all God's children.

Anyone looking to grow toward a more fulfilling career and balanced life will benefit from this book. Thanks again, Fred, for being a *Solutionary* to the many.

—**Anthony Bouquet**
Solutionary and author of *The Bloodline of Wisdom: The Awakening of a Modern Solutionary*

This book is a God-inspired gift to anyone looking to enter or re-enter the workforce. Fred offers practical and common-sense tips that even those who have been working for a while can use to integrate Christian principles into their daily work lives. Fred's blending of

Scripture and stories from a highly successful career as a business leader creates the perfect how-to guide for living a fulfilling Christ-centered life in business and at home. I wish I had read this book when I entered the workforce three decades ago.

—**J. Scott Davison**
Chairman, President, and CEO, OneAmerica

Having spent my entire professional life (forty-five years) counseling people on career and life issues, I was intrigued to read what Fred Sievert, a former president of one of the largest companies in the United States, felt were the top tips to achieving success in work and career. The tips are born from his broad work experience and wisdom and his Christian beliefs and values. I can say without hesitation that they are spot-on. I would encourage all who want to make the most of their giftedness and life to listen carefully to what Fred is recommending.

—**Steven Darter**
President, People Management SMD

Author of *Lessons from Life: Four Keys to Living with More Meaning, Purpose, and Success* and *Managing Yourself, Managing Others: Learn How to Improve Effectiveness, Productivity, and Work Satisfaction*

America's greatest natural resource is its young people, and this book shows them how to maximize their God-given talents. It's another home run by Fred Sievert.

—**Jack Krasula**
President of Trustinus, LLC
Author and WJR radio host of *With God, Anything Is Possible*

Fred Sievert has written a book that inspires, while at the same time offering practical and sage career advice in bite-size chunks. It is an excellent, timeless resource for young professionals who want to become thoughtful, successful leaders who positively impact the world around them.

—**Douglas Campbell III**
The Success Coach (www.thesuccesscoach.com)
Executive & Career Coach; Top 30 Global Guru Coach
Author of Two Coaching Books

I enjoyed reading Fred's book very much, even though preachers are more inclined to speak of callings rather than careers and currently resonate with the phrase "Servant Leader." But many of us are also aspirational. We worry about getting noticed ("Does anybody know I'm out here...see my potential...appreciate what I can do?") Career mobility is something that even preachers think about a lot. Or their spouses may think about it for them. Fred's book, with its excellent tips, will find a very receptive and appreciative audience among many of my colleagues. It will also be a resource that we can make readily available to lay leaders, recent college graduates, and parishioners.

—**William A. Ritter**
Pastor Emeritus
First United Methodist Church, Birmingham, Michigan

As a pastor who first began my working career in the corporate world, I find Fred's book to be extremely relevant—not only for those beginning their careers, but also for those who may find themselves re-evaluating their path in life and how their work correlates to their faith. This book provides practical guidelines for anyone having vocational questions of how their Christian values apply in a secular work environment. The stories of Fred's own personal experience validate the advice he offers. His wisdom on how to integrate one's belief system with a corporate culture will prove enlightening and valuable. I highly recommend this book.

—**Rev. Rebecca Mincieli**
Senior Pastor, John Wesley United
Methodist Church, Falmouth, Massachusetts

FAST-STARTING
A CAREER OF
CONSEQUENCE

Practical Christ-Centered Advice
for Entering or Re-entering the Workforce

FRED SIEVERT

NASHVILLE

NEW YORK • LONDON • MELBOURNE • VANCOUVER

FAST-STARTING A CAREER OF CONSEQUENCE
Practical Christ-Centered Advice
for Entering or Re-entering the Workforce

© 2021 by Fred Sievert

Published in New York, New York, by Morgan James Publishing. Morgan James is a trademark of Morgan James, LLC. www.MorganJamesPublishing.com

Unless noted otherwise, all Scripture quotations are from the Holy Bible, New International Version®, NIV® Copyright © 1973, 1978, 1984, 2011 by Biblica, Inc.® Used by permission. All rights reserved worldwide.

Scripture quotations marked ESV are from the ESV® Bible (The Holy Bible, English Standard Version®), copyright © 2001 by Crossway Bibles, a publishing ministry of Good News Publishers. Used by permission. All rights reserved.

Scriptures marked KJV are taken from the King James Version (KJV), public domain.

Printed in the United States of America

Author photos by Lisa Mancuso-Horn

ISBN 978-1-63195-358-3 paperback
ISBN 978-1-63195-359-0 eBook
Library of Congress Control Number: 2020920439

Morgan James is a proud partner of Habitat for Humanity Peninsula and Greater Williamsburg. Partners in building since 2006.

Get involved today! Visit
www.MorganJamesBuilds.com

DEDICATION

This book is dedicated to my grandchildren, Mia, Aly, Hope, and twin boys, Joshua and Caleb, whom I love dearly. I pray they all will benefit from this book on their spiritual journeys and as they enter the workplace.

TABLE OF CONTENTS

FOREWORD

What a difference a pandemic makes! I'm writing this during the COVID-19 pandemic, in Portland Oregon, as the world shifts and we shift with it. We're pivoting in our understanding of the meaning of work and career, and what it means to be part of a community, as our very sense of self and security have changed. What does it mean to have a career when we're holed up in our homes, working primarily on Slack? What sort of career trajectories will be available in a world shaped by an unexpected crisis? How will I stand out, or have anyone notice what I do when I'm in my apartment, or just one of dozens on another Zoom call? With millions losing their jobs, what does it mean to "fast-start" your career, or re-enter the workforce after massive disruption?

My friend, Fred Sievert, former president of New York Life, a Fortune 100 company, had no forewarning of what was coming when he wrote *Fast-Starting a Career of Consequence*, but it comes at an opportune time, when so many are experiencing anxiety around the future of their careers. Whether you're a young person just finishing college and launching into a first job, reengaging after a layoff, or feeling stuck mid-career, this book is for you. As someone in full-time ministry, I also see the applicability for pastors, youth pastors, and even lay leaders as they minister to their congregations.

In the best of times, unaffected by global pandemics, there can be inherent tensions for committed followers of Jesus as we think about our careers. If our priority is to help build the Kingdom and put others before ourselves, are we supposed to worry about our careers at all? After all, Jesus Himself challenges us not to worry about tomorrow, as each day has enough worry of its own. We're enjoined to consider the birds and the flowers of the field, that take no care for their future, as they have a Heavenly Father to provide for their needs. Our culture and our own ambitions can fuel an unhealthy focus on "getting ahead," perhaps even at the expense of others—a focus that can create or at least accept a false identity for ourselves that says our worth is measured by our accomplishments, who we know, what we own, and how much recognition we gain.

Thankfully, there is another side to the story. As followers of Jesus, we see in Scripture that our talents and abilities, our vocations, and indeed our very lives are given to us by God. We are therefore stewards of these most precious gifts and can see our everyday work as a gift back to a God, who loves us and created us to bless and serve others, and to build into and support God's good creation, including the company, nonprofit, or venture we're working for. We can be devoted to learning how to celebrate and accelerate the unique gifts we've been given by our Creator and joyfully throw ourselves into our work and careers, not from a place of anxiety or a need to impress others, but out of gratitude. We can desire to advance and grow in ways that build others up without sacrificing the other vital parts of our lives.

Fast-Starting a Career of Consequence is full of practical strategies that will help you enter or re-enter the workforce, or set yourself apart as someone with the vision and desire to advance in your current work environment. The very fact that you've bought this book and read this far sets you apart as someone willing to invest time and money to improve your ability to serve and make a difference in the marketplace. The book's foundation rests on biblical principles anyone can apply in the workplace, and it moves on to enumerate practical, strategic, and easily accessed tips for fast-starting a career.

I first met Fred when I was working on the biggest project in my thirty-five years working for the Luis Palau Association: NY CityFest. I had thrown myself headlong into a nearly five-year effort to bring together more than fifteen hundred New York City churches from across the metro area to love and serve their neighborhoods and share the Good News of Jesus. In response to an invitation from hundreds of leaders, we aimed to mobilize thousands of Jesus followers to pray, serve, and share the Gospel in more than one hundred events, eventually culminating in celebrations in Times Square, Radio City Music Hall, and Central Park. It was by far the hardest thing our organization had ever tried to do, with a budget that kept climbing. Not only was I travelling back and forth from my home (and headquarters for LPA) in Portland Oregon, I'd been warned that the sheer scale, complexity, and diversity of NYC was beyond belief. The warnings proved true. Despite working on similar projects in hundreds of world-class cities for decades, there were times when we wondered what we had gotten ourselves into.

Of the hundreds of amazing leaders I had the privilege of meeting over the course of those years, Fred stood out in a number of ways. His calm demeanor. His eagerness to support and encourage others. He listened far better than most leaders I've been around. I could tell any advice he gave me was going to be worth gold, based as it was on the principles he'd learned and refined over decades spent leading major companies. He supported the NYC effort financially, certainly, but his friendship and advice have meant far more. To have a book I can now share with people who are standing at the crossroads of their work lives is a blessing.

As I read the book, I found myself looking back at the early years of my own career. Granted, my "career path" is pretty unusual. In fact, if you don't count strawberry picking during my summers as a middle-school and early high-school student, I've worked at only one place: the nonprofit my evangelist father started almost sixty years ago. That came with its own challenges, of course. When I started at LPA back in 1985, the day after I graduated from Wheaton College, one of my primary concerns was the perception of nepotism. Surely everyone would be looking at me and thinking, "This kid only got this job because his dad started the organization." That's a lot of pressure on a twenty-two-year-old who'd also just gotten married. (Now that my wife, Michelle, and I have three adult kids, that seems pretty young!) I had no choice but to stumble along, on my own, unsure of who to ask for help, and whether the doubts I was dealing with were normal. Thankfully, the good example of my dad, who was always a hardworking and biblically sound leader, helped. I moved my way along by trial and error, gradually working my way up in the organization as needs arose or someone left to pursue another opportunity.

Many of the lessons I learned in those days came back to me as I read this book, including these: demonstrate strong commitment to the organization; fully understand the vision, mission, and culture; be prepared for meetings; learn how the business works, even outside your own scope of responsibility; develop your skills as a speaker and presenter; and earn the trust of your peers. I wish I had had this book back then, and I recommend it to you now.

Wherever you are on your work and career journey, I pray that you'll put God first and throw yourself into developing a career that offers you personal fulfillment and joy, allows your gifts to be well exercised, and provides a platform to honor the Lord.

Let the journey begin!

Kevin Palau

President, Luis Palau Association

Portland, Oregon

ACKNOWLEDGMENTS

The support and encouragement of my family and friends, as well as my extensive network of business associates (all too numerous to mention by name) is what inspired me to complete this book in the face of many other pressing priorities.

The book is a culmination of much work by an entire team of extremely competent individuals who made my work much easier and more enjoyable.

Writer, researcher, and editor Libbye Morris, added significantly to the book's readability and relevance by identifying and succinctly articulating research findings that strengthened the impact of many elements of the book's advice.

Social media expert Becca Ryan maintained and expanded my platform to readers around the globe who will benefit not only from this work but also the numerous daily postings of related and relevant spiritual stories and advice on our website, "Stories of God's Grace."

I must also thank the following readers of the draft manuscript and trusted friends who provided welcomed and extensive constructive criticism of the initial draft manuscript that served to greatly enhance the book's relatability and readability: The Reverend Joanne Swenson; The Reverend William Ritter; The Reverend Rebecca Mincieli; literary agent Greg Johnson; and fellow executives J. Scott Davison, Larry Barton, Larry Ward and Steven Darter.

And finally, I am grateful to all the fine folks at Morgan James Publishing who immediately recognized the value of the combination of spiritual and business advice contained in *Fast-Starting a Career of Consequence.*

PART 1
INTRODUCTION
AS WE BEGIN...

Is it possible to advance within a secular organization as a strong Christian who regularly professes his or her faith? Does it seem unlikely that the president of a Fortune 100 company could achieve that level of success while freely and openly expressing his or her Christianity?

For me, not only was it possible; it was only through my personal relationship with Jesus Christ, my awareness of my God-given spiritual gifts and my reliance on the daily guidance of the Holy Spirit that such career advancement could ever have occurred.

This book is about the symbiotic relationship between faith and career. As Christians, we are happiest and most pleasing to God when we identify our God-given spiritual gifts and then use them in service to the Lord and in pursuit of our chosen careers.

To set the stage for the advice that is given in this book, let me start with the genesis of the book.

Advice to My Daughter Was the Genesis of This Book

The genesis of this book was a question my daughter, Dena, posed to me after she had graduated from college with a degree in French. She found entry-level employment in the marketing department of a large international cosmetics firm. She was essentially languishing in that position, fulfilling marketing orders. She came to me in near desperation and asked, "What can I do to get noticed and distinguish myself from all the other young employees?"

I thought long and hard about how a new employee at my own company might get a fast start and thereby become recognized as someone of high potential. As a result of fully thinking that through, I initially came up with five tips that I shared with Dena. They are reflected in chapters 6 through 10 of this book.

Dena, who is also a strong Christian, had enormous success after following these tips, remaining true to her faith and applying biblical principles in the workplace. After observing her success, I decided to use the same tips in mentoring young students, family and friends. Later, I used them as the theme of four commencement addresses I delivered at colleges, universities, and even at one high school. The feedback I've received from those who took the advice and acted on it has been overwhelmingly positive and very gratifying to me.

Little did I know at the time that this would result in a spiritual calling that would fulfill my passion of positively impacting lives for Christ through my faith and my business experiences. Writing this book has been a perfect way to do exactly that.

After these early successes, I realized that getting noticed in a large organization can be a daunting task that frustrates many recent graduates, as well as older adults who are re-entering the workplace.

Even if they excelled in their undergraduate studies or in their prior assignments, individuals starting in a new position often ask how they can be noticed or be labeled as "high potential" by their new company and management team. So often, they embark on what they believe is an exciting new opportunity, only to find themselves languishing in a low-level administrative role that provides little or no satisfaction.

They often wonder when the career they hoped for would really get launched. Even business school graduates don't often know how they can become noticed by senior management. This can lead to disappointment, frustration, and a feeling that their expensive education never really panned out the way parents, instructors, and friends had claimed.

In my business career, I was involved in recruiting and managing hundreds of individuals entering the workforce with diverse backgrounds, educational credentials, and life experiences. They almost always entered or re-entered the workforce with enthusiasm and high expectations.

Unfortunately, many had previously become disenchanted or discouraged as their hopes and dreams of future fulfillment and success waned. The mundane routine of holding positions in which they felt unnoticed and unappreciated often left them unmotivated. Their daily work experience ultimately morphed into pure drudgery.

This situation exists today for many employees with a variety of skills and expertise. It is true for the highly educated as well as the less educated. It is even true for those with MBA degrees from highly respected business schools.

This realization then led me to think even more about success factors for those who are entering or re-entering the workplace. I added five more important tips to my original list of five. This new list of ten tips, coupled with the all-important adherence to biblical principles, should propel any Christian reader who diligently follows them to a high likelihood of early career success.

About the Christ-Centered Career Advice in This Book

I referred earlier to a symbiotic relationship between faith and career. This book is structured to leverage that relationship.

Following the introduction to this book, Part 2 (chapters 1–5) discusses the application of Biblical principles in the workplace. These chapters will help you create a strong foundation for fulfillment in your career. The principles offered in these chapters will add a spiritual dimension to your career pursuits that will be very edifying and impactful.

Part 3 of this book (chapters 6–15) elaborates on practical steps you can take to rapidly gain visibility and early success as you enter the workforce for the first time, move to a new company, or re-enter the workforce after a period of absence. The ten fast-start tips in these chapters are practical strategies you can implement immediately to generate and maintain your excitement and enthusiasm for a job you have just landed—or one you've been in for a while. These tips, based on my own experience as the former president of a Fortune 100 company, can make all the difference as you launch into a new and exciting phase of your vocational experience; linked inextricably to your personal faith.

This book will arm you with advice that will enable you to quickly become noticed and recognized as a high-potential employee who is capable and ready for future advancement and expanded levels of responsibility. In the process, your strong personal faith can positively impact the lives of others who watch your ascension to higher levels within the organization.

Here are just a few examples of common situations you may find yourself in as you seek to enter or re-enter the workplace. If any of the following situations sound familiar to you, you will benefit greatly from the tips in this book:

- As a recent college graduate, you may have chosen an academic major well-aligned with your interests, but you wonder how it can be used in a meaningful role in business that could lead to future success and fulfillment. In this book, you'll find ways to succeed, whatever your college major. It is not uncommon for people to become highly successful in fields unrelated to their areas of concentration during their college years.

- You may be considering a change in your career to a profession or occupation that you feel is a better match for you but might not adequately compensate you for your efforts. Perhaps your passion is in a discipline that typically doesn't compensate well. If you follow the proven fast-start tips in this book that lead to increased responsibilities and management roles, coupled with the application of the Biblical principles in chapters 1 through 5, you can have the best of both worlds: a Christ-centered career that utilizes your spiritual gifts and provides compensation that more than adequately rewards you for your efforts.

- You may be one of those unfortunate millions who either lost their jobs or were placed on furlough during the COVID-19 crisis. Your re-entry into the workforce may be with the same company or with a new company. In either case, it's a perfect time to establish yourself as someone of high potential with a promising future. This book can be a perfect enabler in your workforce re-entry.

- You have decided to re-enter the workplace after several years of child rearing. If so, you are probably anxious about doing so and feel ill-equipped to succeed after years outside the workforce. Perhaps more than others, you need fast-start tips and coping techniques for dealing with the stress and pressure on re-entry.

- If you recently ended your service to our country after a long or even a short stint in the military, you likely enter the workplace with high expectations, but also with a heightened level of trepidation. You may wonder how you'll succeed when so many of your friends and classmates have a head start on you. Equipped with the strength of your faith and the drive, determination, and discipline you undoubtedly learned in the armed forces, you are, in fact, well-prepared to leverage that experience using the fast-start tips in this book to achieve great personal and professional fulfillment.

- If you are a senior pastor, an associate pastor, a youth minister, or even a lay leader in your church, you might be wondering how you can better serve members of your church who are anxious or stressed out over a major life transition like entering or re-entering the workforce. In fact, all the tips in chapters 6 through 15 apply equally to you in your ministry. Just read the titles to those chapters in the table of contents to confirm the applicability of the advice they provide.

In addition to inspiring and motivating you, this book will enable you to accomplish the following:

- Apply biblical principles in all dimensions of your life, including the workplace.
- Get noticed in the workplace, even in a low-level starting position in a large organization
- Develop pertinent skills and knowledge more rapidly than otherwise possible, even without a mentor or participation in a formal training program. As you'll learn in chapter 3, you can think of Jesus as your workplace partner, as I did.
- Become recognized as a high-potential employee with strong strategic capabilities
- Enter management ranks more rapidly if you aspire to do so and have identified leadership or management among your spiritual gifts.
- Compete effectively for early promotional opportunities across a broad range of functions and responsibilities

This book also:

- Enumerates easily implementable actions in each chapter to leverage the advice for fast-starting your career
- Provides you with numerous coping techniques for balancing faith, family, and career while working in an increasingly competitive and demanding workplace.
- Includes relevant Scripture references that relate to biblical principles applicable in the workplace.
- Enables you to determine your unique combination of spiritual gifts using the Spiritual Gifts in the Marketplace Assessment tool (in Appendix A).
- Provides the ways in which Jesus demonstrates leadership and management skills for those aspiring to emulate Him in such roles in the future (in Appendix B).
- Elaborates more on the author's faith journey and testimony (in Appendix C).
- Offers a supplemental workbook for easy future reference and for readers to track their progress in implementing the actions steps provided in the book. The workbook is ideal for group study, as well.

Every life, including yours, is a journey that is important to God. As such, every life is one in which He will provide guidance, blessings, and unconditional love. This applies not only to your worship experiences and your family life, but also to your career. Each one of us is endowed with a unique combination of spiritual gifts that we should consider foremost in making future vocational and avocational plans and decisions.

As you read this book, may God richly bless you and encourage you to implement its advice enthusiastically.

Now, let's begin your journey to a more fulfilling, Christ-centered career by looking at some biblical principles to apply in the workplace.

PART 2

FIRST THINGS FIRST: APPLYING BIBLICAL PRINCIPLES IN THE WORKPLACE

CHAPTER 1

IDENTIFY AND USE YOUR SPIRITUAL GIFTS AT WORK

"For just as each of us has one body with many members, and these members do not all have the same function, so in Christ we, though many, form one body, and each member belongs to all the others. We have different gifts, according to the grace given to each of us. If your gift is prophesying, then prophesy in accordance with your faith; if it is serving, then serve; if it is teaching, then teach; if it is to encourage, then give encouragement; if it is giving, then give generously; if it is to lead, do it diligently; if it is to show mercy, do it cheerfully."

—Romans 12:4–8

Start by Identifying Your Spiritual Gifts

Each of us has a unique combination of spiritual gifts. Discerning what those gifts are and then using them in Christian service is perhaps the most successful approach to choosing work that will lead to sustainable happiness and fulfillment.

Whatever your vocational calling is, you can use your spiritual gifts effectively. As you determine how best to use your unique combination of gifts, you can take comfort in knowing that you are serving the Lord in the workplace.

You will have become a vital part of the body of Christ. And as Paul tells the Corinthians, we need to do "everything in love."

> *"Be on your guard; stand firm in the faith; be courageous; be strong. Do everything in love."*
> —1 Corinthians 16:13–14

The word "everything" is intended to encompass all aspects of our earthly existence, and most of us spend more than half our waking hours at work.

If you have already completed a spiritual gifts assessment exercise and discerned your spiritual gifts, then you are off to a fast start on your pathway to career success. If you have not done so in the past, I strongly encourage you to take the time now to complete the "Spiritual Gifts in the Marketplace" assessment questionnaire in Appendix A. It can be quite enlightening. The results will enhance the effectiveness of what you read in the remaining chapters of this book.

Once you have completed that assessment and you feel you have a better understanding of your own unique combination of gifts, I can assure you that Jesus is eagerly awaiting your invitation for Him to guide you on your working journey. Read more about Jesus as a workplace partner in chapter 3.

Once I fully understood the nature and extent of my own spiritual gifts, I spent considerable time exploring and identifying how I could best deploy those skills and gifts in Christian service in both my business life and my personal life. After all, for Christians, those two dimensions of our existence are inextricably linked and can't be bifurcated, although many people compartmentalize their Christianity and their vocation.

The assessment tool in Appendix A is only a recommended first step in the process of discernment. Once you identify the top several gifts you scored most highly on, think about your own involvement and attitude toward each. Do the activities you undertake in each area give you great satisfaction? Are you good at them? Do people compliment you on your success in those areas? Have you impacted other lives in a positive way through activities associated with those skills? The answers to such questions are likely to narrow your number of discernible and manageable spiritual gifts to three or four.

In my case, it became clear to me that God had given me the gifts of a strong faith, strategic leadership (most often using my financial acumen), and generosity in giving my time and resources.

During my working life and into my retirement years, I used and effectively deployed those gifts in my personal, vocational, and spiritual pursuits. The gifts manifested themselves in ways that were not discernably different as a Christian; as a businessman; or as a friend, father, and husband. I realized that I was not a Christian at times, a businessman at other times, and a father, friend, or husband at still other times. No, I was all these things all the time.

Although that may seem obvious, it was a revelation for me. I could apply my gifts in all aspects of my life because I could not separate my Christianity from my vocation or from my social and family situation. Many Christians overlook that simple but important reality.

Before I came to this revelation while in my late twenties, I felt that worship was a Sunday-only activity and had no role in the workplace. I never prayed at work, and I talked about my faith only with my friends and acquaintances from church.

Does this sound familiar to you? If it does and you are entering the workplace for the first time, coming to this realization will enable you to magnify your impact along all dimensions of your life and accelerate your advancement and success within your chosen career. You will be way ahead of where I was on my Christian journey when I first entered the workplace at age twenty-two.

I have applied my spiritual gifts in all aspects of my life, but what follows in this chapter is specifically how I applied them to opportunities that arose in the workplace.

It is also important to note, as you read about specific examples of my own application of spiritual gifts in the workplace, that the ultimate benefits impacted non-Christians as well as Christians. In all my examples, it was broadly known that I was a Christian and that I gave credit to the Lord for those gifts that enabled Him to reach more people through me.

Applying Your Spiritual Gifts in the Workplace

The following is not meant to prescribe a formula for how you can apply your spiritual gifts in the workplace. The spiritual gift assessment tool in Appendix A identifies twenty-three different spiritual gifts, and there probably are more. Each of us as a human being is unique, and we are each uniquely gifted by God. We all have a different number and combination of those gifts. That makes it difficult, if not impossible, for me to provide advice on how every reader of this book might apply his or her unique combination of gifts.

So instead, I will use my own situation as an instructive example of how you can discover how to use your spiritual gifts in your own work environment. I will elaborate on the three gifts that apply specifically to me. I hope you will follow a similar thought process in considering ways in which you can use your gifts in the workplace.

As I have noted, in my case, it became clear to me that God had given me the gifts of a strong faith, strategic leadership, and generosity in giving my time and resources.

I had determined that I possessed these gifts well before I completed the spiritual gifts assessment tool in Appendix A of this book. But that tool clearly confirmed my own intuitive assessment and allowed me to intently focus on how I might apply those gifts in the workplace.

How did I know I possessed those gifts in advance of doing a formal assessment? Let me mention briefly how I came to that realization over time for each of the three identified gifts. For each one, I then indicate how I applied them in the workplace.

My first book, *God Revealed: Revisit Your Past to Enrich Your Future* (Morgan James, 2014), is a collection of thirty-one personal experiences in which I palpably felt God's presence in my life in ways that, to me, were undeniably providential rather than coincidental. Fifteen of those thirty-one encounters with God occurred in the workplace, and they demonstrate how I used my own personal spiritual gifts.

The Gift of a Strong Faith

At the age of twelve, I had what I have called a "mystical adolescent experience." I told this story more fully as the first story in chapter 1 of *God Revealed*.

It was a warm summer day, my parents were at work, and my brother was outside playing with his friends. I lay on my bed, home alone and contemplating some questions that, at the time, didn't seem to be deeply theological, but later proved to be exactly that:

"Is God real? Does He exist now or only in the past? Can He hear my prayers, and will He answer them? Does God know who I am? Is He watching over my every move and protecting me? Are there really angels? When people say God speaks to them, are they lying or delusional? Does God really speak audibly? Why can't *I* hear God? And why do so many bad things happen in the world—often to such good people?"

About Jesus, I wondered what it meant to be the Son of God. I asked myself, "How can God be a single divine being, yet be in three forms (God the Father, Jesus the Son, and the Holy Spirit)—the Holy Trinity?"

My list of questions seemed endless.

I was not attempting to induce a mystical state, nor did I have any expectation of meeting God. I was simply engaged in deep contemplation over the questions and curiosities that consumed my young mind. While in this meditative state, however, I felt totally at peace—removed from the confines and constraints of my body. I could best describe it as an "out-of-body" experience, although that description seems inadequate. I felt weightless, as if I were suspended above the floor of my room. I felt the love, warmth, peace, and joy of knowing God at that moment.

But these surreal sensations were dwarfed by something else: a vivid connection with the Divine. No physical vision of God, no verbal communication, but an awareness of His presence that was unlike any I had ever felt before. Enveloped and embraced by a bright, warm light, I was filled with an indescribable love. I felt that God was communicating with me that He was real and present among us, then and forevermore. I was assured that the answers to my questions would come in time.

The experience gave me a strong and enduring faith and a burning desire to learn more. After learning that several other ministers and lay leaders in their churches had a similar experience, it occurred to me that this may be God's way of calling those who might later become clergy or lay leaders in their faith communities. Perhaps it is part of God's plan to grant this gift of faith to the inquisitive young minds of those who are receptive to a future divine calling.

In fact, Saint Augustine tells of a similar experience in his famous *Confessions*. Decades later, while attending divinity school, I read about Augustine's fourth-century experience; it felt eerily like God was speaking to me over the span of seventeen centuries.

Appendix C, "The Author's Faith Journey," elaborates more on my quest to deepen my relationship with Christ.

The strong and enduring faith that resulted from that adolescent experience was my first realization of a spiritual gift—the gift of a strong faith.

Applying a Strong Faith in the Workplace

My mystical adolescent experience gave me an unwavering faith that I relied on throughout my career. I believed with great assurance that the Holy Spirit was guiding me in difficult decisions. It was not unusual for me to pray ten or more times every working day.

These were never prayers asking for strong sales or profit results or greater compensation or the next promotion. No, they were more about acting with integrity, being a strong role model for my employees and colleagues, and seeking guidance in making many extremely difficult decisions that were not always as simple as answering the question, "What's the right thing to do?"

Often, these were prayers I said silently in the middle of an important meeting when issues were being discussed and debated that required immediate action. I would simply call on the Lord to help me. I often found myself praying silently, "Lord, I'm not smart enough to deal with this. Please help me come to the right conclusion and to communicate my recommendation or decision in a convincing way."

One of the most wonderful and effective short prayers I say when faced with a tough decision is, "Lord, I can't. You can, please do."

Here is how Jesus responded to the disciples when they asked why they could not heal the boy who had seizures:

"Truly I tell you, if you have faith as small as a mustard seed, you can say to this mountain, 'Move from here to there,' and it will move. Nothing will be impossible for you."
—Matthew 17:20b

Over the course of my thirty-year business career, Jesus moved a lot of mountains for me. He can do the same for you if your faith is strong.

The Gift of Strategic Leadership

I have always been good at math. When I was a child and someone asked me what my favorite subject was, I would instinctively respond with, "Mathematics." Later, I majored in mathematics as an undergraduate in college, earned a master's degree in statistics, and then went through the rigors of intensely difficult actuarial examinations as I began a career in insurance.

I understood that this is a God-given talent because math was always easy for me, and I enjoy the challenge of problem solving. I observed many of my friends and acquaintances struggling with math, or even saying they hated it.

As early as my high-school years, I tutored other students in mathematics free of charge because it gave me great personal satisfaction to help others who were struggling. As an aside, I married one of those students, and we recently celebrated our fiftieth wedding anniversary.

You might ask why I am describing this as a spiritual "gift of strategic leadership." Let me explain how I used my financial acumen in positions of leadership for strategic purposes.

In college, when I joined a fraternity, I experienced my first taste of using those skills as the treasurer, and later as the president, of the fraternity. During those years, I learned that prudent financial management and discipline were necessary to avoid the serious consequences of running a business or an institution that was failing financially. This was the first indication to me that my spiritual gift of strategic leadership would provide me with opportunities to use my financial acumen to benefit others in ways that went well beyond academic mathematics. As a leader within that fraternity, I worked hard before I graduated to develop and implement strategies that would leave the fraternity in a sound financial position that was sustainable for many years.

On my Christian journey, in all the various churches I have attended, I wanted to use my spiritual gifts. So I either volunteered or was asked to serve as a lay leader in a variety of roles: a deacon, a trustee, one of the leaders of a capital campaign, and often as the chairperson of the Finance Committee. Many churches need sound financial management and strong financial discipline to survive, and ultimately to thrive.

Throughout my career and into retirement, I have served on many corporate boards, nonprofit boards, and industry-related committees and task forces. In almost every case, I have been asked to serve as the chair of the board, the chair of a committee, or the chair of a task force. I am certain that strategic leadership is a God-given gift that many others recognized in me, in many cases even before I did.

But how did this gift manifest itself during my career in business? I hope my explanation will enhance your own thinking about how you can apply your spiritual gifts in the workplace when it isn't immediately apparent.

Applying the Gift of Strategic Leadership in the Workplace

I am convinced that God gives each of us gifts we can use in all facets of our lives. I also believe that He presents us with opportunities to use those gifts in ways that may not be immediately obvious to us. We need to seize those opportunities and respond to God's calling.

Here are just two examples of opportunities related to my work life. I am now certain they were in God's will for my life, even though initially I resisted both. Even though these opportunities emerged later in my career and they aren't the kind of thing that might surface for you as you enter or re-enter the workplace, I provide them as examples solely to show how our God-given spiritual gifts may be used at any time in our lives and in either our vocational or avocational pursuits.

The first example surfaced as an opportunity I couldn't refuse in the year 2000, when the chairman of the board of New York Life was ending his term as a trustee of The American College of Financial Services. He asked me to replace him as the New York Life representative. I was reluctant to do so and was thinking of a list of others on the New York Life team who could do a better job than I could. But I knew it wasn't wise to say no to the chairman of the board. I took the post, not realizing that God had opened this door for me because my spiritual gifts were needed at the college.

I served on that board for many years, becoming the chairman of the Budget and Finance Committee and later serving as the chairman of the board in 2006 and 2007—leadership positions once again. At that time, the college owned a large property in Bryn Mawr, Pennsylvania, with many outbuildings and a significant amount of expensive deferred maintenance. Every year, the college was showing a deficit and was at extreme risk of not being able to make payroll. They had no way of dealing with the increasing levels of rising costs.

As the chair of the board, I led a strategic planning exercise that was designed to develop survival strategies as we faced an existential financial threat to the institution. After considering numerous alternatives, it became clear to me that the only viable strategy was to monetize the real estate asset by selling the campus and leasing back only the buildings that we absolutely needed. Ultimately, we had to convince all other board members to agree to this unpopular and somewhat severe action.

We executed the plan at the peak of the real estate market, which provided funds to sustain the college for several years. This move also provided an opportunity to invest the proceeds at the bottom of the equity markets following the financial crisis of 2007–08. That fortuitous timing provided outstanding equity appreciation for several years.

The college now has a strong balance sheet, with more than $90 million in total assets. When we sold the property, the college's total assets were dangerously low, at around $15 million. I am convinced that God was using me (and many others) to solve this existential crisis in a way that now allows the college to impact many hundreds of thousands of lives under a strong and sustainable business model.

The second example is similar in many regards. As an executive at New York Life Insurance Company with an actuarial background, I was asked to join the board of the Actuarial Foundation in 2005. I resisted this offer initially because I had a big responsibility at New York Life and didn't want to dedicate a lot of volunteer time to the organization. I agreed to join the board because I had friends on the board, and I felt a deep gratitude for the career I enjoyed as a result of my actuarial education. I wanted to give back. Little did I know at the time that it would be a forum in which I could very effectively use my spiritual gift of strategic leadership.

After joining the board, I soon realized that although the foundation was following an admirable mission, it had a limited impact by attempting to improve math education nationally by using actuaries to mentor students in selected high-school and middle-school classrooms. At the time, the foundation was mentoring only twenty-five or thirty classrooms across the country and was thereby impacting a total of no more than one thousand students.

During my term as the chair of the foundation board in 2008 and 2009, with the help of the other trustees and a talented staff, instead of impacting only one thousand students nationally, we made a positive impact on millions of students and many thousands of teachers. In a strategic planning session that I led as its chair, the Board of Trustees identified financial literacy as the biggest shortcoming in education across the United States. We identified several strategies to use the resources of the foundation to address this issue. We did so by publishing monthly math-related articles in *Scholastic Magazine* and by developing a world-class financial literacy curriculum for teachers to use in thousands of high schools across the country.

These two examples were tangential to my specific role at New York Life. However, as the CFO of the largest business unit of the company, and later as the president of the company, it was my spiritual gift of strategic leadership that enabled me to enjoy a career that presented many opportunities to use those spiritual gifts.

The Gift of Generosity

I was raised in a lower-middle-income family. Both my parents worked multiple jobs to make ends meet and provide for the family. As a result, I greatly appreciated the value of hard work and of always acting with the highest integrity. The values I learned as a youngster were largely instilled in me by the kitchen-table instruction of my mother and the examples set by both my parents. I was blessed by, and am grateful for, such an austere upbringing.

One of my fondest memories, and something that profoundly influenced my life, is told in chapter 5 of my first book, *God Revealed*, in a story titled "Doing What's Right." It is the story of a struggling family whose young son (me) had a life-threatening accident due to the negligence of a delivery truck driver. The accident caused me to be hospitalized for a few days, and doctors were concerned that I had potential brain damage. Despite the strong recommendation of a plaintiff's attorney, my parents refused to sue the driver's company. They insisted that God would reward us and richly bless us for not getting greedy over the potential for instant wealth.

They were right.

Being raised in the Detroit area, I was well aware of the poverty around us. My mother often reminded my brother and me of how fortunate we were, even though we could hardly be described as children of privilege or affluence. She reminded us often that we should always try to help others less fortunate, to the extent we could.

I have always tried to honor her wishes. As a result, I have been blessed and gratified that I had the capacity and willingness to give generously.

This value was instilled in me before I ever read the story of the widow's mite. Jesus's words continue to inspire me to give more:

> *"Calling his disciples to him, Jesus said, 'Truly I tell you, this poor widow has put more into the treasury than all the others. They all gave out of their wealth; but she, out of her poverty, put in everything—all she had to live on.'"*
>
> —Mark 12:43-44

Early in your career you aren't likely to have the capacity to give significant sums to the charities of your choice. However, even if you are currently living paycheck to paycheck, I'd strongly recommend, like the widow in the biblical story, that you begin to develop the discipline of giving generously to others less fortunate and to worthy charitable causes.

One of my favorite passages in the New Testament is when Jesus tells the parable of the separation of the sheep from the goats:

> *"Then the righteous will answer him, 'Lord, when did we see you hungry and feed you, or thirsty and give you something to drink? When did we see you a stranger and invite you in, or needing clothes and clothe you? When did we see you sick or in prison and go to visit*

you?' The King will reply, 'Truly I tell you, whatever you did for one
of the least of these brothers and sisters of mine, you did for me.'"
—Matthew 25:37–40

My wife and I financially support numerous charities, churches, and faith-based organizations. Our giving is entirely out of gratitude for the many blessings that have been bestowed on us and out of a strong desire to compound our effectiveness in spreading the Good News of the Gospel. We have a passion for, and a personal commitment to, helping others less fortunate than ourselves. For us, that practice began when we were newlyweds, living paycheck to paycheck.

Applying the Gift of Generosity in the Workplace

How can this gift of generosity manifest itself in the workplace? And how can you make that assessment or determination? Generosity can take many forms, but here's what you should look for.

As a new or re-entering employee, internally your company (or the one you are hoping to join) may be considered generous in the compensation and benefits it provides employees.

However, you should consider other evidence of their generosity. Look carefully at how the company extends its generosity externally by encouraging employees to give their time, talent, and financial resources to worthwhile causes, nationally, regionally, and within the communities in which the company's employees live and work. Matching charitable financial gifts is a common practice of many corporations.

The company's leaders can support and encourage volunteerism by employees. They might even grant employees time off on workdays to volunteer in their communities. If the company has a stated articulation of its corporate values, see if what it is doing in this respect is consistent with those stated values.

If you are blessed with the spiritual gift of generosity, these are ways in which you can serve the Lord by using that gift in the workplace. Ideally, the company in which you work will support those efforts.

In my experience at New York Life, some of my most memorable and gratifying moments were in overseeing the millions of dollars in grants made annually by the New York Life Foundation to worthy nonprofits in hundreds of communities around the country. During many award ceremonies at which I presided, I was often moved to tears as I heard the stories of the dedicated and sacrificial work of individuals who had a strong passion for the missions of their nonprofit organizations.

Even the leaders of many large public companies are now suggesting that their typically heavy focus on shareholder value needs to shift to a broader focus on stakeholder value. Stakeholders can include customers, employees, community residents, and even social causes.

I thanked God often for the blessing of working for a company that, in so many ways, afforded me the opportunity to use my unique combination of spiritual gifts.

Another Approach to Determining Your Giftedness

If you are interested in learning more about the biblical connection to giftedness, I found the following excerpt from the book *The Power of Uniqueness: How to Become Who You Really Are* by Arthur Miller, Jr., and Bill Hendrix to be useful. My own personal interest was strong enough to encourage me to undertake the extensive Motivated Abilities Pattern® (MAP®) analysis that Art created, and it fully confirmed my own giftedness in areas even beyond my spiritual gifts.

MAP is an individual's unique design, or giftedness—his or her unique set of abilities. It is something that makes us tick and determines our successes and failures.

Miller developed a process called the System for Identifying Motivated Abilities® (SIMA®) to help individuals discover their MAP. The process is composed of three steps:[1]

1. Recall and summarize your achievements.
2. Describe in detail what you did.
3. Make an inventory of recurring themes.

God and Our Giftedness

Here is what Arthur Miller says about God and our giftedness:

If we believe in God, then it is impossible to escape the conclusion that God is the originator of our individual giftedness. So much in our life is determined by our giftedness that it is impossible to believe that God, who according to the Bible cares about what happens to each one of us and has a purpose for each one of us, is not involved in our design and our giftedness.[2]

Besides, it is what Scripture teaches. Here is Miller's summary of what you can find in the Bible:[3]

- God has created you (Gen. 1:27).
- God has designed you in order to fulfill his purpose for your life (Rom. 12:6).
- God's Spirit can dwell within you and actively seek to work his purpose out through your design (John 14:26).
- God will hold you accountable for fruit produced from your giftedness (Matt. 16:27).

- God intends that you use your giftedness in work appropriate to its nature and within its boundaries (Rom. 12:6–8).
- God requires you to love him and those you serve, with excellence and with passion (qualities only available through your design!) (Matt. 22:36–38).
- God promises He will bless you and complete his intention for your life (Rom. 8:28).
- God has instructed us to build his kingdom on the earth as it is in heaven using the giftedness with which we were endowed (1 Cor. 12:4–7).

These daunting expressions of God should fill you with excitement and fear and disbelief and hope—all at the same time. God is serious about you and your life. God has a game plan for your life…if you are willing.[4]

———

I hope the examples in this chapter of my experience in identifying and using my spiritual gifts will enable you to identify your own gifts. Once you identify them, thoughtfully consider the ways in which you can deploy them in your workplace environment.

CHAPTER 2
ALWAYS ACT IN CONCERT WITH YOUR VALUES AND BELIEFS

"For God so loved the world that he gave his one and only Son, that whoever believes in him shall not perish but have eternal life."
—John 3:16

People tend to expect companies and their leaders to have, and espouse, specific sets of beliefs and values. In chapter 7, we will discuss the importance of understanding and embracing your company's mission and vision statements. These important documents articulate a company's purpose for existing and aspirations for the future. It's hard to imagine how a company could move forward without a specific set of guidelines to inform decisions.

It is equally important for you, an *individual*, to have a specific set of beliefs and values to guide your decisions. Without knowing the values that define you and your character, you will have no reference point for determining which companies align with your personal values and beliefs and which companies do not.

If you are looking for a new position or attempting to re-enter the workplace, as you begin to interview with various companies, look at their websites and read their value statements to find out what is important to them. Ask questions during your interview. You are interviewing the potential employer, just as its recruiters are interviewing you.

What Are Your Core Beliefs?

As Christians, regardless of our chosen faith denomination or tradition, we share some common core beliefs. However, each individual has his or her own unique perspective, so your own personal list will be somewhat different than someone else's. The important thing is to identify a specific set of core personal beliefs. I highly recommend that you construct your own short list of beliefs using the advice below to assist you in the exercise.

Perhaps the most fundamental and universal statement of Christianity is embodied in a single biblical verse: John 3:16. As you articulate your own beliefs that apply to all facets of your life, remember to include your Christian beliefs.

One way to ponder variations of statements of belief is to read several Christian creeds. The oldest creed of the Christian church is called "The Apostles' Creed." It serves as the basis for others that followed. There are several versions. I particularly like this one because it is a reflection of my own beliefs:[5]

I believe in God, the Father Almighty, Maker of heaven and earth, and in Jesus Christ, His Only Son, our Lord, who was conceived by the Holy Spirit, born of the virgin Mary, suffered under Pontius Pilate, was crucified, died, and was buried; on the third day, He rose from the dead; He ascended into heaven, and is seated at the right hand of God the Father Almighty; from there He shall come to judge the living and the dead. I believe in the Holy Spirit, the holy catholic church, the communion of saints, the forgiveness of sins, the resurrection of the body, and the life everlasting. Amen.

Just about every church and Christian organization has its own set of core beliefs, sometimes expressed as a "Statement of Faith" or "What We Believe." As you try to succinctly encapsulate your own beliefs that apply to the workplace, I recommend visiting some of the websites of companies that espouse Christian values and beliefs and reflect on some of their beliefs that might resonate with you.

What Are Your Core Values?

Here are just three examples of companies' values statements that could facilitate your thoughtful approach to establishing your own short list of values:

1. Starbucks:

Starbucks is not a company known for Christian values, but I included this example because everyone is familiar with Starbucks, and the company has countless loyal customers. Also, you can see that values should be specific and meaningful, regardless of the extent to which they embrace Christian values.

Here is the company's values statement:[6]

With our partners, our coffee and our customers at our core, we live these values:
- Creating a culture of warmth and belonging, where everyone is welcome.

- Acting with courage, challenging the status quo and finding new ways to grow our company and each other.
- Being present, connecting with transparency, dignity and respect.
- Delivering our very best in all we do, holding ourselves accountable for results.

We are performance driven, through the lens of humanity.

2. Hobby Lobby

Hobby Lobby is known as a Christian company that abides by Christian principles consistently. Here is the company's core values statement:[7]

From the beginning, the company's core values have formed a foundation to guide decision making, establish the corporate culture and determine how business is conducted. Hobby Lobby's values include:

- Honoring the Lord in all we do by operating in a manner consistent with Biblical principles
- Offering customers exceptional selection and value
- Serving our employees and their families by establishing a work environment and company policies that build character, strengthen individuals and nurture families
- Providing a return on the family's investment, sharing the Lord's blessings with our employees and investing in our community

While retail strategies change, Hobby Lobby's core values remain. These values led to the decision to close all stores on Sunday allowing associates time for family and for worship. They were also instrumental in the decision to give store employees pay raises well above the national minimum wage.

3. In-N-Out Burger

In-N-Out Burger is known for its Christian values. The company prints Bible passages on its cardboard cups, containers, and wrappers. However, interestingly, the company does not mention its Christian values on its website or in its core values. The core values, established in 1948 and never revised, are "to serve only the highest quality product, prepare it in a clean and sparkling environment, and serve it in a warm and friendly manner."[8]

Company spokesman Carl Van Fleet told *USA Today* in 2005 that the founders' son, Richard Snyder, instituted the practice of printing Bible passages on their materials, saying, "It's just something I want to do."[9]

You can see from that list of company values statements how much they can differ.

I recommend that you articulate your own list of personal values. Your values define what is important to you, what you will not tolerate, and who you are. Many websites offer word lists, step-by-step strategies, questionnaires, and quizzes that can help you discover your personal core values.

To build your list, career website Indeed.com suggests asking yourself these questions:[10]

1. What kind of culture do I want to work in?
2. What things, settings, or resources are necessary for me to do my best work?
3. What qualities do I feel make strong, healthy relationships?
4. What qualities do I admire most in my role models?
5. What motivates me?
6. What qualities do I wish to develop in myself professionally and personally?
7. What are my future goals? What qualities will it take to achieve them?

It's important to identify and clearly articulate your own core values.

Core Values That Employers Look For

Each employer is different, but there are some common characteristics that company leaders consider valuable in new hires.

According to one career-advice website, the top five values that employers look for are a strong work ethic, a positive attitude, honesty and integrity, a motivation to learn, and professionalism.[11]

Those characteristics fall into the category of "soft skills"—personality traits—as opposed to "hard skills," which are technical or industry-specific skills. It is well known among business leaders that you can teach people technical skills, such as how to operate software, but it is next to impossible to teach someone integrity, honesty, work ethic, coachability, and other important "soft skills."

According to Susan Peppercorn, CEO of Positive Workplace Partners, "Employers want to know that you are qualified for a position, but they also want to see that you will fit in with the company culture. The only way to assess this is to get a sense of your personality. Knowing that someone has the experience and skills to be successful in a job is paramount, but when two candidates have similar capabilities, often the soft skills are why one person gets hired over another."[12]

The Apostle Paul, in his letter to the Colossians, referred to some important characteristics and behaviors that would reflect Christian values. As you construct your list, be mindful of the importance of these behaviors that Paul alludes to:

"Therefore, as God's chosen people, holy and dearly loved, clothe yourselves with compassion, kindness, humility, gentleness and patience."

—Colossians 3:12

As you build your list of core values to adhere to in the workplace, it's important that they reflect and align with your Christian beliefs. Be on the lookout in the workplace for worldly values that overshadow your Christian values.

According to the Christian Bible Reference Site, the values taught in the Bible are often the opposite of worldly values: kindness and respect for all people instead of power, humility instead of status, honesty and generosity instead of wealth, self-control instead of self-indulgence, and forgiveness instead of revenge. Additional Christian values include kindness to all people, humility, honesty, living a moral life, generosity with time and money, practicing what you preach (not being a hypocrite), and a willingness to forgive others.[13]

Again, it can be helpful to review the values statements of companies mentioned earlier. The corporate value statements on their websites can inform your decision in establishing your list of personal values that apply in the workplace.

How Beliefs and Values Impact Workplace Behaviors

Identifying your personal values impacts your workplace experience in two ways:

1. First, once you have completed this exercise, you will be equipped to determine how consistent various corporate strategies, actions, or decisions are with your personal beliefs and values.

   You will undoubtedly encounter situations in which your beliefs and values are not perfectly aligned with your company's beliefs and values. This doesn't necessarily mean you should consider resigning from the company or lodging a whistleblower complaint; the way you react will depend on the nature of the issue. If something is going on that is illegal or unethical, you will need to decide if it is serious enough for you to take action.

2. Second, and perhaps more importantly, clearly articulating your own personal beliefs and values allows you to be constantly mindful of the need for you to maintain your moral compass. It provides for greater self-awareness. It gives you criteria and standards for decision making and for assessing your own performance to see how consistent it is with your company's established beliefs and values.

We all need to be personally aware of the need to act at work in a way that honors our core beliefs and exhibits the values we most admire in others and in ourselves.

Challenges in the Current Business Environment

CEOs and managers who are not willing to adapt their business practices to weather today's fast pace of change are sometimes tempted to cut corners to increase their position in the marketplace while their competitors invest in upgrading and expanding their processes.

Unethical behavior in the workplace has become more commonplace as pressures build for individuals to achieve aggressive goals. Much of this behavior is driven by a desire to maximize incentive compensation that is based on the achievement of those aggressive goals. Superiors often exert pressure on employees—even those in entry-level positions—to cut corners or to act unethically. Identify such pressures and maintain your moral compass, even if it means risking your future in the current company by communicating your concerns and refusing to compromise your own personal ethics to benefit the company.

Call on the Holy Spirit to guide you and to help you overcome even the slightest temptation to engage in wrongdoing.

"No temptation has overtaken you except what is common to mankind. And God is faithful; he will not let you be tempted beyond what you can bear. But when you are tempted, he will also provide a way out so that you can endure it."
—1 Corinthians 10:13

Persecution of Christians exists throughout the world. And it seems that will never change. As Christians, we have a moral duty to uphold our Christian beliefs, despite the fact that many people reject us and our religious beliefs and values. Adhering to your Christian values in the workplace, despite the repercussions, is part of living a Christian life.

If you are encouraged to engage in activities that are against your personal values and beliefs, take a stand. Pray for guidance. Seek out the counsel and support of other Christians. Talk with someone at work whom you trust. In some situations, the only solution is to leave the job. But it would be better to stand up for your principles and lose your job than to succumb to corporate greed and immorality and weaken your bond with your Savior, Jesus Christ.

CHAPTER 3
JESUS AS A WORKPLACE PARTNER

"Come to me, all you who are weary and burdened, and I will give you rest. Take my yoke upon you and learn from me, for I am gentle and humble in heart, and you will find rest for your souls. For my yoke is easy and my burden is light."
—Matthew 11:28–30

As Christians, we all know how important it is to live according to Christian principles, and to put our trust in Jesus Christ, as we navigate our personal lives, relationships, and difficulties. It might not seem as obvious to rely on our faith as we navigate our careers. But it is important to do so. Our careers represent a significant part of our lives and our identities. Considering Jesus as a workplace partner can make work-related decisions and challenges much easier.

Being Yoked to Jesus

Throughout my career, I felt Jesus was an omnipotent, omniscient, omnipresent workplace partner. I love the imagery of being yoked to Jesus (as noted in Matthew 11:28–30) while tackling the heavy lifting of difficult issues and challenges. In sharp contrast to that imagery is the warning from the Apostle Paul in 2 Corinthians 6:14 to avoid being yoked to, or partnering with, unbelievers. This doesn't mean we can't engage or work with others (even non-believers)—and as a result, have a positive influence on them—but as Christians, our values have to come from being yoked to Jesus.

> *"Do not be yoked together with unbelievers. For what do righteousness and wickedness have in common? Or what fellowship can light have with darkness?"*
> —2 Corinthians 6:14

There are many examples of business partnerships gone bad (despite good intentions) due to fundamental differences between partners in their beliefs, values, and practices. Being yoked to Jesus makes it easier to adhere to your values and to choose workplace partners who share those values.

In the sections that follow, we will explore what the Bible says about work and the workplace and what Jesus Himself said to assure us that He will be with us in all aspects of our lives, now and forever.

Jesus is indeed the best possible and most powerful imaginable workplace partner or companion. As you read the Bible verses that follow, think about, and watch for, your own opportunities to emulate Jesus.

We must always remember, however, that we are not on an equal level with Jesus; no humans are. We strive to serve Him, to live in a way that will please Him, and to use our spiritual Gifts to honor and glorify Him.

If you aspire to greater leadership or management roles and feel that you have spiritual gifts in this area, Appendix B, titled "What You Can Learn from the Bible and Jesus About Leading and Managing" contains a number of examples of key traits and characteristics that Jesus exhibited. They are worthy of your emulation.

A highly respected friend of mine and a successful businessman, J. Scott Davison, is the chairman, president, and CEO of the insurance group OneAmerica. He told me the one piece of advice he gives to people aspiring to future leadership roles. It is great advice and is applicable to all facets of your workplace experience, whether or not you aspire to greater leadership roles. Here's exactly how he expressed it: "My response is always, 'Get over yourself,' meaning once you stop trying to achieve for your own sake and just start humbly and relentlessly serving the organization and those around you, you'll be shocked at how much success will come your way."

Examples of Company Leaders Guided by Jesus (through the Holy Spirit)

CEOs who live out their faith in the workplace set the example for everyone in their businesses. Culture begins at the top. When the CEO acts in ways that reflect Christian values and expects everyone else to do the same, it can permeate the entire organization.

One example of a CEO who relies on his Christian faith to run his business is David Morken, the founder and CEO of Raleigh, North Carolina-based Bandwidth, which provides communications-related services globally. The company recently hit the $2 billion valuation mark. Morken says his Christian faith has helped him get through the tough times. Back in 1999, the young attorney turned entrepreneur, fresh from serving in the Marine Corps as a judge advocate, cofounded Bandwidth from a friend's spare bedroom. His success didn't happen overnight, but he refused to give up in the face of multiple challenges. Morken says, "I crawl under my desk and pray often. That's me."[14]

Christian CEOs in the sports world have the opportunity to impact countless people, from their players to their fans.

An example of a sports CEO who lives out his Christian beliefs in his job is Clark Hunt, the CEO, chairman, and co-owner (with his mother, Norma), of the Kansas City Chiefs. Hunt was named chairman of the team in 2005. On January 19, 2020, he led the Chiefs to win Super Bowl LIV. It was the Chiefs' first Super Bowl victory in fifty years.[15]

Christian believers on the Chiefs team typically get together every other Monday for Bible studies, led by Marcellus Casey, the team's chaplain. In the playoffs, the importance of prayer became the focus for the group. Chiefs long snapper James Winchester noted after the Chiefs' Super Bowl win in 2020, "It's hard to find a word that describes how important prayer is for us. It is a huge help to us in our daily walk. It's huge to be able to bow your head and talk to the heavenly Father. It is something I'm thankful we have, the gift that He's given us."

The following is a list of just a few high-profile Christian business leaders (some still living, some now deceased) who have achieved phenomenal success while operating their businesses in concert with their Christian beliefs:[16]

- Mary Kay Ash, founder of Mary Kay Cosmetics
- S. Truett Cathy, founder of Chick-fil-A
- Carl Karcher, founder of Carl's Jr. restaurants, and Andy Puzder, the current CEO
- John Willard Marriott, founder of Marriott Hotels
- David Neeleman, founder and former CEO of JetBlue
- James Cash Penney, cofounder of J.C. Penny retail stores
- Dave Thomas, founder of Wendy's restaurants

- John Tyson, founder of Tyson Foods
- Sam Walton, founder of Walmart stores

Many of these successful leaders struggled along the way and came from humble backgrounds. Here are a couple of notable examples.

Dave Thomas, the founder of the highly successful Wendy's fast-food chain of restaurants, was often quoted as saying, "You can be anything you want to be within the laws of God and man."[17]

Although Thomas was a billionaire at the time of his death in 2002, his origins were humble. His mother put him up for adoption shortly after his birth, and then his adopted mother died when he was five. After a stint in the US Army and a series of restaurant-related jobs, he started working with the legendary Colonel Sanders of KFC fame. Putting the lessons he learned from this estimable personage into effect, Thomas opened the first Wendy's in 1969 in Columbus, Ohio.[18]

S. Truett Cathy, the founder of Chick-fil-A, was born in 1921. He and his siblings grew up helping their mother in the kitchen of the boarding house she ran. For a dollar a day, a boarder received a bed and two meals—breakfast and dinner. Cathy shucked corn, shelled peas, set the table, and washed dishes, cleaned bathrooms, and made beds. Their father sold insurance policies, but in those Great Depression years, his income was never enough to pay ordinary family expenses. When Cathy and his brother, Ben, were older, they both had paper routes in their West End neighborhood in Atlanta. Cathy often used his own paper-route money to pay for groceries. Then, in 1935, when the brothers became the primary breadwinners with their paper routes, the Cathys left the boarding house and moved into Techwood Homes, the nation's first federally subsidized housing project.[19]

On May 23, 1946, the two brothers opened the Dwarf Grill (later renamed the Dwarf House) in Hapeville, Georgia. With four tables and ten stools at the counter, their first-day sales totaled $58.20.[20]

Stories like these are truly inspiring. Through perseverance and determination, it doesn't matter how or where you start out; you can achieve success simply by continuing to strive for what you believe in, abiding by your values along the way.

What the Bible Says about Work

Throughout the Old Testament and the New Testament, there are numerous scriptural references to the importance of work and conducting it in a responsible, trustworthy, and reliable way. Of course, in biblical times, the work environment was considerably different than it is today, but the human condition was not. We can still learn from biblical wisdom in conducting our own business affairs.

The following Scriptures can help you exhibit and honor your Christian faith in your work life. It's amazing how relevant they are today, so many centuries later.

In the very beginning, God put Adam to work:

"The Lord God took the man and put him in the Garden of Eden to work it and take care of it."
—Genesis 2:15

And labor will be rewarding:

"You will eat the fruit of your labor; blessings and prosperity will be yours."
—Psalm 128:2

Jesus Himself exhibited humble servant leadership:

"Jesus knew that the Father had put all things under his power, and that he had come from God and was returning to God; so he got

up from the meal, took off his outer clothing and wrapped a towel around his waist. After that, he poured water into a basin and began to wash his disciples' feet, drying them with the towel that was wrapped around him."
— John 13:3–5

Perhaps the most succinctly stated wise advice to us today was written by the Apostle Paul to the Colossians almost two thousand years ago:

"Whatever you do, work at it with all your heart, as working for the Lord, not for human masters, since you know that you will receive an inheritance from the Lord as a reward. It is the Lord Christ you are serving."
— Colossians 3:23–24

And the Apostle Peter reminds us to use our spiritual gifts in service to others:

"Each of you should use whatever gift you have received to serve others, as faithful stewards of God's grace in its various forms."
— 1 Peter 4:10

What Jesus Says about Work

Although many of the verses below don't address workplace matters directly, they are words Jesus spoke that, as a Christian, you need to be mindful of in your work life.

Your primary objective in the workplace should be to serve the Lord, not to amass wealth:

"What good is it for someone to gain the whole world, yet forfeit their soul? Or what can anyone give in exchange for their soul?"
— Mark 8:36

If your priorities are well-aligned with Jesus's teachings, you will be rewarded:

> *"But seek first his kingdom and his righteousness, and all these things will be given to you as well."*
> —Matthew 6:33

Jesus wants to see you thrive and grow:

> *"His master replied, 'Well done, good and faithful servant! You have been faithful with a few things; I will put you in charge of many things. Come and share your master's happiness!'"*
> —Matthew 25:23

Don't restrict your prayer life only to Sundays or only to your house of worship. Pray often at work:

> *"Therefore I tell you, whatever you ask for in prayer, believe that you have received it, and it will be yours."*
> —Mark 11:24

Earn trust through honesty and integrity:

> *"Whoever can be trusted with very little can also be trusted with much, and whoever is dishonest with very little will also be dishonest with much."*
> —Luke 16:10

Fruits of the Spirit–Confirming Your Success

As Christians, we rely on the Holy Spirit to help us become more and more like Jesus. It is a lifelong journey that probably will never be fully achieved. But if you are mindful of the goal and you are constantly striving to achieve it, your happiness and success will essentially be assured. We can periodically assess our progress by remembering what the Apostle Paul said were the fruits of the spirit in his letter to the Galatians:

> *"But the fruit of the Spirit is love, joy, peace, forbearance, kindness, goodness, faithfulness, gentleness and self-control."*
> —Galatians 5:22–23

In what the Bible says and what Jesus Himself says, we have a model for success in any endeavors we pursue. As it relates to the message of this book, be intentionally and constantly mindful of the fact that the model applies to all aspects of your life—especially in the workplace, where you spend most of your waking hours.

As you read the specific advice provided throughout the remaining chapters of this book, remember that Jesus is not only your Lord and Savior, but He also can be a powerful and helpful workplace partner through the advice and guidance of the Holy Spirit. On a daily basis, share your workplace challenges and issues with Him, and ask for guidance.

CHAPTER 4

PRAY OFTEN FOR GUIDANCE FROM THE HOLY SPIRIT

"And I will ask the Father, and he will give you another advocate to help you and be with you forever—the Spirit of truth. The world cannot accept him, because it neither sees him nor knows him. But you know him, for he lives with you and will be in you."
—John 14:16–17

In chapters 6 through 15 of this book, the focus is on practical tips and advice you can take to add value at your company, even in the early years of your tenure. In many of those chapters, implementing my advice can lead you to make observations and discoveries you need to communicate to people in positions of authority who can effect change. In those chapters, I often advise you to prayerfully ask the Holy

Spirit for guidance in decision making and in how best to deliver those communications.

In this chapter, I want to explain why I consider prayer such an important biblical principle to be applied—not only in your personal worship, but also in the workplace and in all other dimensions of your life.

As Christians, nothing is more central to our beliefs and our ability to emulate and follow Jesus than the concept of the Holy Trinity and the importance of the Holy Spirit, who dwells within us.

In business, we often need to make difficult decisions, and we stress about the right thing to do. Even in cases in which an ethical response is called for, the best decision is not always easily discernible. There often seem to be nuanced considerations.

Making the "right" decision often becomes a difficult task, and then communicating a decision can be equally difficult but no less important. The most effective and convincing words don't always flow naturally from our lips.

As indicated in John 14, the Father will give you an advocate, and you need to trust in that assurance. I hope you will find, as I have, that prayer and the guidance of the Holy Spirit are essential elements of your successful entry or re-entry into the workplace.

Recent Research on How Prayer Enhances Our Well-Being

Christians, as well as followers of other religions, understand the benefits of prayer in strengthening their spiritual well-being and connection to God. But research shows that prayer benefits our mental, emotional, and physical health as well. Studies have shown a direct relationship between spirituality and positive health outcomes, including those related to mortality, physical illness, mental illness, health-related quality of life, and the ability to cope with illness, including terminal illness.

For example, one study found that prayer frees up cognitive resources needed to focus on mental tasks by reducing the extent to which people are distracted by negative emotions.[21] Entering or re-entering the workforce can be a stressful time, filled with anxiety, uncertainty, and worry. Prayer can help alleviate those negative emotions.

The benefits of prayer are so significant, in fact, that there is an entire new field of science devoted to understanding the types of changes that take place in our brains when we engage in religious experiences or practices. It's called *neurotheology*, or the neuroscience of religion.

At the forefront of this research is Andrew Newberg, MD, a neuroscientist at Thomas Jefferson University in Philadelphia. He says, "When prayer elicits feelings of love and compassion, there is a release of serotonin and dopamine." He explains that both of these neurotransmitters play a role in how you feel. Serotonin has a direct impact on your mood, and not having enough serotonin has been linked to depression. Dopamine, on the other hand, is associated with reward and motivation. Newberg and his colleagues found that in following a retreat centered on prayer and meditation, people experienced beneficial, long-term changes in their dopamine and serotonin levels. He believes that both prayer and meditation can result in permanent changes in the brain regarding these neurochemicals.[22]

There is evidence that the benefits associated with praying are greater if you believe God is a loving, caring Creator, as opposed to viewing God as a strict, angry disciplinarian.

Researchers from Baylor University found that people who pray to a loving and protective God are less likely to experience anxiety-related disorders—worry, fear, self-consciousness, social anxiety, or obsessive-compulsive behavior—compared to people who pray but don't really expect to receive any comfort or protection from God. For people who view God as a source of comfort and strength, prayer allows them to enter into an intimate relationship with Him and begin to feel a secure attachment. When this is the case, prayer offers emotional comfort, resulting in fewer symptoms of anxiety disorders.[23]

Prayer also helps us form and maintain social bonds. Researchers in one study found that prayer helps promote the value of sacrifice and the strength of relationships. In our personal and professional lives, being willing to compromise and make personal sacrifices is critical to healthy relationships. Sacrifice promotes trust, which strengthens relationships.[24] Building trust is an important element in fast-starting your career of consequence.

Other studies have found that prayer inspires forgiveness and reduces anger and aggression.[25]

Research shows that prayer enhances our physical health as well.

For example, researchers at the Mayo Clinic concluded, "Most studies have shown that religious involvement and spirituality are associated with better health outcomes, including greater longevity, coping skills, and health-related quality of life (even during terminal illness) and less anxiety, depression, and suicide. Several studies have shown that addressing the spiritual needs of the patient may enhance recovery from illness."[26]

Intercessional Prayer for Others Is Beneficial to Us

In chapter 15, you will read about some of my own longstanding daily practices, or "coping techniques," I've used to balance faith, family, and career. One of those techniques is daily prayer, in which I spend time in intercessional prayer for others in need.

I have kept a daily prayer list for many years. Every morning, I go through the list and pray individually for all those on the list. The list is a diverse collection of people ranging from immediate family members to colleagues from work to national and local leaders, and even strangers I may have met only once but who shared their prayer needs with me.

It is especially important to pray for people you interact with at work. Work-related relationships are often strained and difficult. But, in addition to praying for improvement in those relationships, pray for nonwork-related personal struggles or illnesses you might learn about that your colleagues in the workplace are facing.

Telling coworkers that you are praying for them or for their family members is perhaps one of the easiest ways to share your faith while letting them know you care. I have much experience in doing this at work. Some of my strongest work-related relationships flourished after committing time in prayer in support of their needs.

There is another very powerful and gratifying outcome resulting from the prayer list practice. Over time, I have marveled at how many of the prayers have been answered. When they are answered, I move them into a category at the bottom of the list called "answered prayers." Daily, I thank God for His faithfulness in honoring those prayers.

My long list is compartmentalized into the following categories, each of which can relate to family members, friends, or work colleagues: serious health issues, financial issues, emotional issues, relationship problems, and finally, answered prayers.

Praying through Conflicts at Work

Whatever the source, conflicts with others at work can be unproductive, debilitating, and disheartening.

If you encounter difficult situations in your workplace that you feel you have no control over, such as working with a difficult person, turn to God in prayer. Pray for insight about how to cope with and improve the situation. Pray for God to heal the rift in your working relationship with the other person. Replace any tendency to direct anger toward that person by instead praying that God will heal whatever is happening in his or her life that makes the working relationship uncomfortable.

You will find that praying for others will have a soothing, calming effect on you and the way you handle difficult situations. In addition, I have found that God often softens the heart of the other person in ways I thought were not possible.

Biblical References to the Power of Prayer and the Role of the Holy Spirit

The Bible mentions prayer and the accessibility to the Holy Spirit through prayer many times in both the Old Testament and the New Testament. As Christians, we believe in the Holy Trinity—God the Father, the Son, and the Holy Spirit. And we know we can have a personal relationship with Jesus Christ.

We are reassured of this reality innumerable times throughout the Bible. We can rest assured that our access to the Holy Spirit is real.

Rather than try to provide a comprehensive list of all such references, I want to highlight only a few that are particularly reassuring to me. But first, I want to mention some of the key verses in which Jesus Himself speaks of the importance of prayer in our lives.

What Jesus Said about the Power of Prayer

Here is just a sampling of some of my favorite verses elaborating on the power of prayer as uttered by Jesus Himself in the four Gospel accounts of Matthew, Mark, Luke, and John.

In His own words, Jesus told us the following in the Gospels about prayer for others—even our enemies:

"You have heard that it was said, 'Love your neighbor and hate your enemy.' But I tell you, love your enemies and pray for those who persecute you."

—Matthew 5:43–44

I think of this verse from Matthew every time I enter into prayer in a church service, a Bible-study class, a men's breakfast meeting, or a meal with my family. Jesus told us He would be with us when we gather in His name. From my perspective, this is extremely reassuring:

> *"Again, truly I tell you that if two of you on earth agree about anything they ask for it will be done for them by my Father in heaven. For where two or three gather in my name, there am I with them."*
>
> —Matthew 18:19–20

In this short passage from Mark, Jesus reminds us of the power of prayer and how important it is to forgive—not only others but also ourselves—just as our Father in heaven has forgiven us:

> *"Therefore, I tell you, whatever you ask for in prayer, believe that you have received it, and it will be yours. And when you stand praying, if you hold anything against anyone, forgive them, so that your Father in heaven may forgive you your sins."*
>
> —Mark 11:24–25

And in the book of John, considered the most theological of the four Gospels, Jesus tells us that things we ask for in His name that glorify God will be done.

> *"And I will do whatever you ask in my name, so that the Father may be glorified in the Son. You may ask me for anything in my name, and I will do it."*
>
> —John 14:13–14

What Jesus Said about the Holy Spirit

In the New Testament, Jesus emphasizes many times the accessibility and importance of the Holy Spirit. Here again are some representative verses from the four Gospels.

This passage from Mark is particularly relevant to entering the workplace. You will need to rely on the Holy Spirit to guide you in constructing the right words in your important communications with fellow employees:

> *Just say whatever is given you at the time, for it is not you speaking, but the Holy Spirit.*
> —Mark 13:11b

In Luke, Jesus reiterates that the Holy Spirit was promised by God and it represents power from on high:

> *"I am going to send you what my Father has promised; but stay in the city until you have been clothed with power from on high."*
> —Luke 24:49

Here is another theologically packed description, from the Gospel of John. It speaks of the existence and nature of the Holy Spirit as described by Jesus Himself.

> *"If you love me, keep my commands. And I will ask the Father, and he will give you another advocate to help you and be with you forever—the Spirit of truth. The world cannot accept him, because it neither sees him nor knows him. But you know him, for he lives with you and will be in you."*
> —John 14:15–17

What the Apostle Paul Told Us about the Holy Spirit

The Apostle Paul, originally a persecutor of Christians, had a "Road to Damascus" encounter with Jesus. As a result, he became one of the most important figures in the history of Christianity and the presumed author of potentially as many as thirteen books of the New Testament. Most of those writings were letters to early Christian communities in the first century AD.

Here are some notable Scripture references from the writings of Paul. In them, he provides assurances about the existence and the power of the Holy Spirit in our daily lives. This is something that will be vitally important to you as you enter or re-enter the workplace. We can learn a great deal about the Spirit in just these four representative verses.

In Galatians, Paul indicates that the Spirit that is sent is the Spirit of God's Son, Jesus:

> *"Because you are his sons, God sent the Spirit of his Son into our hearts, the Spirit who calls out, 'Abba, Father.' So, you are no longer a slave, but God's child; and since you are his child, God has made you also an heir."*
>
> —Galatians 4:6–7

Paul tells the Philippians very clearly that their prayers for him and the indwelling of the Holy Spirit of Jesus, as provided by God, will deliver him:

> *"For I know that through your prayers and God's provision of the Spirit of Jesus Christ what has happened to me will turn out for my deliverance."*
>
> —Philippians 1:19

And writing from prison to the Romans, Paul speaks from his heart. While he is mired in a difficult existence, he expresses how the Spirit gives him hope and triumph, even in his suffering:

"Not only so, but we also glory in our sufferings, because we know that suffering produces perseverance; perseverance, character; and character, hope. And hope does not put us to shame, because God's love has been poured out into our hearts through the Holy Spirit, who has been given to us."

—Romans 5:3–5

Pray Often To, and Rely Heavily On, the Guidance of the Holy Spirit

During my career, I relied heavily on daily prayer in the workplace, sometimes ten to fifteen times per day. Such occasions could occur in the midst of a tough meeting or phone call. I firmly believe that the Holy Spirit dwells within me and provides me with the appropriate decisions and words to express them.

I strongly urge you to apply the important biblical principle of praying to and relying on the Holy Spirit for guidance on a daily basis at work. Often, when faced with a difficult business or ethical decision, the only thing I knew for sure was that I wasn't smart enough to make the best decision alone, without guidance. And, as a Christian, who better to guide me than the Spirit of the Lord, dwelling within?

You might think it odd that I'd make that statement about ethical decisions. But the truth is, ethical decisions are not always black and white. It is not always as simple as answering the question, "What is the right thing to do?"

After retiring from New York Life, in addition to attending divinity school, I also taught a business school course on leadership, strategy, and business ethics at Fairfield University in Fairfield, Connecticut. In preparation for the course, I developed a curriculum that included sixteen business case studies and fifteen ethical dilemmas that I personally experienced during my career. In those situations, I was the primary decision maker, responsible for the outcome.

In every one of those situations, in the heat of managing through them, I turned often to the Lord in prayer for advice and guidance on the business-related strategic, tactical, and ethical issues. I listened intently for answers—not only about what decisions I should make, but also about how to communicate those decisions to the interested parties.

I had complete faith that the Holy Spirit would provide such advice, and I was never disappointed.

As you begin a new career, you might not be in the ultimate decision-making role for a number of years. But as you advance in the organization and take on management responsibilities, you can be sure you will face many difficult decisions.

However, this advice is just as important to you if you have no management responsibilities or if you are in a technical role that doesn't often face major business decisions or difficult ethical dilemmas.

When you have read chapters 6 through 15 and you begin to implement those fast-start tips, you will most certainly find yourself needing to make decisions on how you use the knowledge you have gained. Also, you will wonder how and when to communicate what you have learned in the process. You will find prayers for guidance to be an essential Bible-based practice throughout your entire career.

Remember, as you've read in the words of Jesus and the Apostle Paul, you have power from on high dwelling within you. The Holy Spirit will provide you with answers relating to the decisions you need to make, the actions you need to take, and the best way to effectively communicate those decisions and actions.

CHAPTER 5

APPLY THE GOLDEN RULE WITH COWORKERS AND CUSTOMERS

"Do onto others as you would have them do onto you."
—Luke 6:31

Almost all of us were aware, as children, of the Golden Rule. However, many children (and even adults) may not be aware that the words "do unto others as you would have them do unto you" were spoken by Jesus Himself in the books of Matthew and Luke.

The importance of this concept to Jesus is evident because He often is quoted in all four Gospels referring to related concepts of loving others: In three of the Gospels, He mentions what He calls the second greatest of the commandments, "to love others as you love yourself." Those references are in Matthew 19:19, Mark 12:31, and Luke 10:27.

In the book of John, considered the most theological of the Gospels, the word "love" is mentioned fifty-seven times, often in Jesus's own words, as in this verse from John:

> *"My command is this: Love each other as I have loved you."*
> —John 15:12

But many times, once we become adults, we forget about the Golden Rule and rarely apply it in the business world. It's a Bible-based principle that, if adhered to in the business world, will serve employees and customers well. It can even create competitive advantage for companies and career-advancement opportunities for employees. My focus in this book is how your awareness and application of this principle can enhance your entry or re-entry into the workplace.

Recent Business Practices Often Ignore the Principle

Increasingly, more and more companies are using artificial intelligence, robotics, big data analytics, online promotions, and other types of automation to expand their market penetration, and thus their profits and growth. But many times, a dependence on automation diminishes the quality of care companies provide to employees and service they provide to customers.

In this high-tech environment, the Golden Rule is more relevant than ever in defining how employers should treat their employees and customers. The "Golden Rule" is the adage that became assigned to the biblical principle of treating others as you would want to be treated yourself.

With constant assaults on our privacy and companies' reliance on machines and voice software, it is more important than ever to gain sustainable competitive advantage (the essential goal of *strategy*) through strong and personal customer service. Millions of consumers are turned off by some of today's "creative" but impersonal and intrusive marketing techniques. By facing and addressing this reality, your company's leaders can help their bottom line greatly by making a concerted effort to follow the biblical principle.

Entering a company as a new employee, initially you won't have decision-making authority to change much of what you read about in this chapter. However, even as a new employee you can distinguish yourself by demonstrating an awareness of these issues and you can begin to position yourself for possible management or leadership roles in the future.

In this chapter, I suggest a number of action steps. You can apply them in stages, as your knowledge evolves over time on issues relating to the application of the Golden Rule.

Today's Lack of Personalized Customer Service Presents an Opportunity

Now that technology is an integral part of the business landscape, sometimes employees' efforts to abide by the Golden Rule are compromised.

Heavily automated processes, which many companies install to reduce operating costs and increase efficiency, can interfere with the human interaction that enhances customers' overall experience with companies. For example, studies have shown that many customers dislike international call centers and robocalls.

It is remarkable to reflect on the changes that have occurred over just the past few decades. These changes demonstrate a strong and rapid movement away from the wisdom of the Golden Rule articulated so succinctly in the Bible almost two thousand years ago.

This situation creates an opportunity for you, over time, to begin to reverse the trend and provide meaningful and constructive input to the management of your own company. However, I would advise you to proceed cautiously and pray for guidance from the Holy Spirit as you begin to make observations and communicate your suggestions to those who can ultimately effect change.

There are many ways for your company to apply the Golden Rule when working with people, depending on the industry, your company's business model, and the type of products the company offers.

The one universal issue and area for meaningful and sustainable competitive advantage is in the company's relationship with its customers and the services it provides to them.

In my opinion, the revolution in online and phone technology, in many ways, has been regressive rather than progressive. This is yet another case in which the simplicity of biblical principles is timeless and overrides technological improvements. The trend toward technology-driven customer service actually creates an enormous opportunity for you and your company.

I don't know how many times I have had an unpleasant experience in trying to access customer service and said to myself, "It is apparent that no one with decision-making authority has tested out this servicing capability that is totally flawed."

Have you ever been frustrated by the absolute inability to contact a live human being while online or on the phone? Sometimes I think this inability is intentionally made difficult. Giving companies the benefit of the doubt, they may not realize that while they enjoy the cost savings from not providing human-to-human customer service, the unintended consequence may be that their customers will often give up in frustration and take their business elsewhere.

Applying the Golden Rule in Employee and Customer Interactions

Just as it is important for your company to follow the Golden Rule in the treatment of employees and customers, it is equally important for you to understand the issues that can surface in your own interactions with fellow employees and with the company's customers.

Here is some advice I encourage you to implement from two perspectives. One relates to interactions as an employee within the company, and the other relates to interactions of various kinds from the perspective of a customer. This is something you can undertake even as a new employee.

Here are some tips for how you—and as a result, your company—can develop and benefit significantly in this regard from your observations. These are simple yet powerful ways to get noticed. Few employees would ever consider doing the potentially time-consuming steps I am recommending. However, if you do, I can assure you it will pay off.

This advice will be even more important to your future as you eventually manage employees and take on new responsibilities. When that time comes, you will be well equipped to use what you have learned if you initially develop the habit-forming practices suggested here.

Interactions or Communications That Naturally Occur in the Workplace

Develop the habit of thoughtfully observing common human interactions in which you are either directly involved or that you witness. The universe of possible situations is almost unlimited. Here are just some common employee-to-employee or company-to-employee internal interactions, some of which can easily go wrong:

- A face-to-face meeting with a superior, a peer, or a subordinate
- An email, voicemail, or text communication
- A corporatewide communication to all employees
- A performance review by your immediate supervisor
- A verbal confrontation in a staff meeting

- A public reprimand of you or someone else
- Gossip or criticism of others in the workplace

After any of these or other situations occur that cause you to experience some level of discomfort or concern, ask yourself the following four questions, and jot down your observations. Few people do this, yet this approach will teach you valuable insights about effective interactions and communications. You don't have to be a psychologist to come to some meaningful observations and conclusions. Most importantly, be mindful of the Golden Rule as you consider your answers to these questions:

1. Is there anything about this experience that could have been handled in a more effective way to generate the hoped-for reaction or response?
2. If you were the person involved in delivering such a communication, how would you have handled it differently?
3. If you were the person on the receiving end, how would you have preferred to be treated?
4. Is this situation serious enough that you feel compelled to comment on it or intervene? If so, what would be the most tactful and effective way to do so?

The key result of this level of observation and thoughtful consideration is that in the future, when you are directly involved in a similar situation, you will have already thought through how to handle it most effectively.

By observing situations like these, you will learn how to better apply the Golden Rule in your interaction with others who work for, and do business with, the company. It's an application of a simple biblical principle for you to embrace and implement in your interaction with others in the organization, whether they are superiors, peers, or subordinates.

You don't necessarily need to talk to anyone about it or suggest that others change their behaviors. However, as your career advances and if you begin to manage others, you will certainly be a more effective coach or mentor after learning what you have from this practice.

Interactions with Customers

Equally valuable is to observe and consider how you'd want to be treated as a customer. Depending on your role in the company, this could be more difficult than observing interactions among employees. The types of situations just mentioned occur naturally within the company, and you will readily observe situations like those almost every day. But you'll need to proactively find ways to observe or participate in customer interactions.

There are two issues that make the customer exercise more difficult. First, if you don't naturally interact with customers as a part of your normal workday, you need to find a way to seek out and observe interactions with customers. Second, if you are going to have an impact based on your observations from the customer perspective, you may need to communicate what you find and your suggestions for improvement to someone who has the authority to make changes.

I caution you that it might be difficult to tactfully communicate weaknesses you uncover in communications to, or interactions with, customers. But finding a tactful way to do it could have a beneficial impact on the company's reputation, on its relationships with its customers, and on your future.

Here are some tips for how to deal with those issues:

1. The easiest way to observe customer interactions is to become a customer yourself. After you become a customer, reach out to

interact with the customer service department with a variety of inquiries or requests. Assess how you are being treated by the service representatives and whether or not that service lives up to the Golden Rule standard.

2. If the company has online servicing capability, explore the service website with the intent of assessing its capability and its user-friendliness. Make note of what you like and don't like about the online experience and think about how it could be improved.

3. Most companies also send periodic mailings and other communications to customers, including annual reports and various forms of marketing materials, to solicit feedback or to sell additional products. Make note of things that are confusing or poorly communicated and consider sharing what you have learned with your immediate supervisor.

4. You can similarly scrutinize the corporate website, and while you're on the site, sign up for periodic email notifications.

5. Perhaps the best source for valuable customer feedback can come from your company's distributors. No matter what type of products your company is offering, someone has to sell them. Distributors of your products are on the front lines and closest to the customer. As a result, they can provide you with the best insights regarding how customers are treated by, and interface with, the company. They might also let you know about issues, weaknesses, and even improvement opportunities for your company's products and services. You will probably need to ask your direct supervisor how you can be introduced to one or more of the company's distributors so you can gain a better understanding of the distribution of the company's products. Just asking that question will impress your boss. More

importantly, following up with the distributors will provide you with valuable insights into customer relationships.

These efforts can require a significant commitment of your time. I don't recommend that you aggressively pursue all my recommendations when you first join the company. However, I highly recommend doing so in a systematic way over time. Keep notes on what you have learned. Even if you don't make a single suggestion to anyone about your findings, your own personal development will be significantly enhanced as a result of this effort.

If you decide that you really should communicate what you have learned, tread cautiously.

Communicating Your Findings Tactfully

Most of the advice given in this book can be implemented early in your tenure with a new company and on a relatively aggressive timetable. But in the case of communicating your critique of interactions with the company's customers, caution is advised. As you advance in your career, I would advise you not to simply communicate problems to your superiors but rather to come to them with solutions to those problems.

However, early in your tenure with a new company, any hint of arrogance, perceived superior intellect, or judgment on the part of an employee who is new to the company can be a major career blocker. Unless your role in the company is directly related to assessing and improving customer relations or services, initially view your observations about customer interactions as early fact-finding. You will get opportunities to slowly roll out your suggestions over time, as your career advances.

Opportunities will naturally surface, either in your capacity as a customer of the company or in your reading of corporate communications to customers. When you are ready to communicate some of your more important observations, here is some advice on how to deliver your feedback appropriately.

1. As a Customer

Your best opportunity to communicate ideas will come after you become a customer.

When you contact customer service (as suggested earlier), either by telephone or online, it is highly unlikely that the service rep will be able to effect significant change.

So you will need to determine where, within the company, to communicate your findings. This will be based on relationships within the company and where you perceive you'll encounter the least resistance.

In any event, be tactful, be measured, and don't approach anyone with a comprehensive list of significant ideas, concerns, or changes. Instead, it is best to indicate that you experienced some difficulties in your interactions with the customer service department and wanted to pass it along. That relatively soft and humble approach is far more likely to produce change than communicating a comprehensive laundry list of ideas. Once you establish such a relationship with a key contact, it will be easier in the future to offer more suggestions.

2. As the Reader of Written Communications

You can take a similar approach after you have read a variety of corporate communications to customers. If you've identified poorly worded or confusing language, then determine what functional area of the company has developed the piece. Again, unless you discover a serious deficiency in communication, be thoughtful about when and how you alert others to what you have discovered. If a change is not urgent, then it would be best to wait until you have a good, well-established relationship with someone in the appropriate functional area.

As a Christian, pray that the Lord, through the Holy Spirit, will provide you with opportunities to present your findings and the wisdom to do so tactfully and at the most appropriate time.

The Golden Rule as a Biblical Principle

In this age of impersonal communications, technological advancements, and fewer direct human interactions than historically has been the case, the Golden Rule is even more relevant and more important than when it was articulated by Jesus in the Gospels of Luke and Matthew.

At work, at home, and in every interaction we have with others, the Golden Rule is a simple and abiding guideline that encourages us to treat others well, show compassion, and "love thy neighbor as yourself"—in essence, the Christian tenet of emulating Jesus in every way.

PART 3
TEN PROVEN FAST-START TIPS

Introduction to Part 3

"Whatever you do, work at it with all your heart, as working for the Lord, not for human masters."
—Colossians 3:23

As you read the ten tips in Part 3, and then begin to implement them, it is critically important to remember that you are indeed working for the Lord, not for human masters. All of the related actions you take, and decisions you make, should be consistent with your personal values and beliefs, as noted in chapter 2.

Some chapters in this book suggest areas of follow-up that could be considered presumptuous and too aggressive if they are not handled with sensitivity and wisdom. I have reiterated this point in the chapters where I believe a note of caution about this is needed. However, my best advice in those areas is to pray for guidance from the Holy Spirit and listen intently for answers.

CHAPTER 6
DEMONSTRATE COMMITMENT

"Commit to the LORD whatever you do, and he will establish your plans."
—Proverbs 16:3

One of the best ways to fast-start your career is to demonstrate commitment. This chapter suggests a few high-impact ways in which you can immediately become more visible and recognized. Always remember the advice in chapter 2: to act in concert with your beliefs and values. The simplicity of the recommendations in this chapter belies their importance. Attention to this short list of easily implementable strategies can be your launchpad for future success in almost any organization. But first and foremost, as we are advised in Proverbs 16:3, "Commit to the Lord."

Some of the strategies discussed in subsequent chapters require more in the way of proactive effort, but no strategy rivals clearly demonstrating commitment to your company by some simple actions and behaviors.

If you have identified your spiritual gifts as discussed in chapter 1, you will have positioned yourself to make intelligent decisions on how to demonstrate your commitment by doing so in concert with your understanding of your own unique combination of spiritual strengths and gifts.

Commitment Is the Key to Thriving as an Individual at Any Company

Many employees with high potential find themselves, at some point in their careers, faced with a choice of being a "small frog in a large pond," as the saying goes—one of hundreds or thousands of employees in a large organization—or being a "large frog in a small pond" in extreme cases by starting their own businesses and making all the decisions.

But now there is a third option, according to David Armano, Executive Vice President of Global Innovation and Integration at Edelman. He calls that third option being an *intrapreneur*. He defines an intrapreneur as "someone who has an entrepreneurial streak in his or her DNA but chooses to align his or her talents with a large organization in place of creating his or her own."[27]

He believes it is important for companies to create a culture of intrapreneurship because it leads to more committed staff members who are given opportunities to grow the organization and make a name for themselves by developing new processes, services, or products. Armano says, "This creates the feeling that their long-term personal success is connected to that of the organization, providing them with powerful motivation to stay with and improve the business."[28]

This is another compelling benefit of demonstrating your commitment to your company—you can be innovative and make a significant contribution within the support system of a large organization.

In my case, by employing my spiritual gifts and through my reliance on the guidance of the Holy Spirit, I ultimately was blessed with a fourth scenario: I became a large frog in a large pond. That's something that not everyone strives for because it comes with significant responsibilities and many challenges. Nonetheless, whether you aspire to that outcome or not, the possibility may very well emerge for you.

If you are entering the workplace for the first time or re-entering after an absence or after a move to a new employer, consider taking the following actions to demonstrate your commitment, starting on day one in your new role. The practices that follow apply, regardless of the size of your company.

Arrive to Work Early, and Leave Late

One of the most noticeable ways to demonstrate commitment to a company is to arrive at work early and leave late.

To understand the typical behavior of many employees, all you have to do is observe how many people enter a company in the few minutes before the workday begins and see how many leave as soon as, or just minutes after, the workday ends. At the beginning of the workday, you are most likely to observe a rush at the official start of the day, with many stragglers coming in late. At the end of the workday, if it's a large company, you will probably witness a near stampede of individuals rushing out the doors at or before the designated close of business.

While it may be difficult for high-ranking executives of the company to notice which employees are coming in precisely at the opening of business, or leaving precisely at the close of business, it is much easier to spot those who are at their workstations thirty minutes before the official workday begins and those who stay well beyond the official closing time. Typically, top executives are on the job early and leave late—so your presence will be noticed by those whom you hope will notice. This is a simple way to demonstrate your commitment, and it will be well worth the additional investment of your time.

Be Passionate about the Company's Mission and Your Role in Pursuing It

Chapter 7 focuses on the mission of a company in more detail, but it also applies to demonstrating commitment, the focus of this chapter. You will distinguish yourself above many other young or new employees if you embrace the mission of your organization and articulate ways in which your work effort is supporting that mission. To be certain that you can honestly embrace the mission, you really need to consider this question before you even accept employment at the company. It is easy to find the corporate mission on most companies' websites. And when you consider your fit with the corporate mission, do so through the lens of your own spiritual gifts, as you discerned in the exercise suggested in chapter 1.

I once met with a CEO of an insurance company (who will remain nameless) who told me he was far more concerned with the bottom line than he was with the quality of customer service or the relationship with his company's vendors. He unashamedly said it was the corporate intent to squeeze as much expense as possible out of the service operations and to extend his payables to vendors as long as possible. Needless to say, I could not work for such a company. At the corporate level, this is clearly a violation of the Golden Rule, discussed in chapter 5.

Your passion for your work and for the mission of the organization will be noticed and can be infectious.

Much has been written about mission-driven organizations, but not as much about mission-driven employees. You can set a standard that few others will naturally exhibit by being vocal about the value of what your company does, as well as your joy in, and gratitude for, being a part of it.

You've heard it said that if you follow your passion, you will never work a day in your life. I have found that to be absolutely true. But it is also true that *demonstrating* your passion can exponentially increase your impact on the organization and that will be noticed and rewarded.

Demonstrate a Strong Work Ethic

"Do you see someone skilled in their work? They will serve before kings; they will not serve before officials of low rank."
—Proverbs 22:29

The term "work ethic" is often used to refer to working longer and harder and putting in extra effort. While that perception is largely true, there is much more that constitutes evidence of a strong work ethic.

Taking the following actions will convey a strong work ethic, not only to superiors in your workforce but also to your colleagues and subordinates. Be sure to demonstrate elements of your work ethic that will also convey your values—the ethics part of the expression "work ethic":

- Complete projects on time and within budget.
- Focus on execution and completion of your daily work assignments.
- Take on difficult tasks with enthusiasm.
- Deliver on your promises.
- Always act with integrity, honesty, and accountability.

As a Christian, you are probably beginning to notice how the biblical principles in chapters 1–5 are inextricably linked to the fast-start principles in chapters 6–15. You will be noticed in a favorable way as you demonstrate a strong work ethic, as suggested in the above behaviors. If you indeed view Jesus as a workplace partner, as suggested in chapter 3, behaviors consistent with the above will definitely please your new partner.

Seek Out More Work

"Let us not become weary in doing good, for at the proper time we will reap a harvest if we do not give up. Therefore, as we have opportunity, let us do good to all people, especially to those who belong to the family of believers."
—Galatians 6:9–10

The Apostle Paul is speaking of the family of believers in Galatia. However, it is a good idea to similarly consider your colleagues in the workplace as important members of your extended "family."

From my own experience as a top-level executive, what impressed me the most about some employees was their willingness and eagerness to do more for the company. They were the ones who accomplished everything I asked of them in excellent and timely fashion and also made it clear to me that they were willing to do, and contribute, more.

To be clear, I am not saying you should ask for a promotion; rather, communicate that you would be happy to help your colleagues or your boss with additional tasks that need to be completed.

Ankit Patel, a member of the *Forbes* Young Entrepreneur Council (YEC), calls this behavior "being hungry," and it is one of the six traits he has identified among top-performing employees. Patel says employees who are "hungry" are those who look for teammates who need help. They have almost no downtime in their day.[29]

Express your commitment not only as a willingness to help the company succeed, but also as a way for you to learn more about the business and contribute to a mission for which you hold a passion.

Be Visible

The genesis of this book, as mentioned in the introduction, was my effort to answer my daughter Dena's question about ways she could increase her visibility in the first company she worked for on a full-time basis after her college graduation.

As simple as it sounds, if you want to increase your visibility, then *be visible.*

Now that you have committed to working added hours each week, as just noted, there might not be time to do all of these things. Choose those activities that make sense for you and that you can fit into your busy schedule.

To increase your visibility, consider doing one or more of the following:

- Help plan, and/or participate in, company and departmental functions and celebrations.
- Be a part of company-sponsored volunteer activities.
- Take lunch and coffee breaks in the company cafeteria, and try to meet employees from other departments whom you haven't previously met.
- Occasionally try showing up at the office for an hour or two on the weekend. You'll almost certainly be noticed as you run into other similarly committed employees.
- Participate in developmental courses or training offered by your company.
- If yours is a publicly traded company, attend the annual shareholder meeting.

Maintain a Positive Attitude

"May the God who gives endurance and encouragement give you the same attitude of mind toward each other that Christ Jesus had."
—Romans 15:5

Maintaining a positive attitude throughout the workday under all conditions can be challenging, but it is imperative. How you conduct yourself under stressful conditions signals how you will handle positions of greater responsibility. Always remember that subordinates, colleagues, and superiors will remember how you react when pressured, challenged, or criticized.

The higher you move up an organization, the more people will notice your moods and attitude. When you are promoted into leadership, you must set a positive example for those you lead. Leaders who crumble under stress are considered to be problematic for their organizations.

In 2018, the leadership training company called VitalSmarts asked 1,334 employees in the United States and Canada to describe their bosses' weaknesses, particularly during stressful times, such as when they must make important decisions and lead key projects.[30]

The authors of the survey analysis state that managers who display the following behaviors tend to "have teams with low morale that are more likely to miss deadlines [and] budgets, and…act in ways that drive customers away." The survey mentioned leaders who:

- Grow impatient with workers who struggle to master complex new tasks but won't offer sufficient training or support.
- Are upbeat and positive with higher-ups when describing progress on a project but are critical and pessimistic with subordinates working on the same project.
- Blurt out remarks that are callous, demeaning, or ridiculing.

- Ask employees for input on projects and then shoot down all their ideas.
- Are unwilling to listen to or support workers when they encounter obstacles on a project.

In chapter 3, I described how it's helpful to view Jesus as a workplace partner. Before giving in to the temptation to exhibit any of the above objectionable behaviors, think about how your workplace partner (i.e., Jesus) would feel about His partner doing so. He would not be happy for a partner to exhibit grievances in public or to engage in any of these other destructive behaviors.

As Paul wrote in his letter to the Romans, your attitude toward others must emulate Christ's attitude toward us.

On a more positive note, the same study mentioned above also noted that when managers under pressure remain calm, collected, candid, curious, direct, and willing to listen, their teams are not only happier and more engaged, but they also tend to accomplish the following:[31]

- Meet quality standards and act in ways that benefit customers 56 percent more often.
- Meet deadlines and have better morale 47 percent more often.
- Improve workplace safety 34 percent more often.
- Meet budget goals 25 percent more often.

This study is just one of many that shows how impactful a positive attitude can be in the workplace—not just in terms of building professional relationships, but also in increasing the bottom line.

I fondly remember a dozen or more people I interacted with regularly during my career who always lifted my spirits with their own positive attitudes. The joy they derived from coming to work and interacting with others at all levels was infectious. In particular, their uncanny ability to agreeably disagree with others in a confrontation that could otherwise get nasty was remarkable. I tried hard to emulate such behaviors.

Always strive to elevate your humility and empathy and to control your temper. Doing so demonstrates a self-awareness and emotional stability that everyone will recognize as mature and professional.

CHAPTER 7

UNDERSTAND AND EMBRACE THE COMPANY'S VISION AND MISSION

I never cease to marvel at the wisdom expressed in the proverbs that were written more than two thousand years ago. The numerous references to plans and vision are just as relevant today as they were then.

> *"Where there is no vision, the people perish: but he that keepeth the law, happy is he."*
> —Proverbs 29:18 (KJV)

> *"The plans of the diligent lead to profit as surely as haste leads to poverty."*
> —Proverbs 21:5

"Many are the plans in a person's heart, but it is the LORD'S purpose that prevails."
—Proverbs 19:21

I have been in planning sessions in which the top management of a company debated how the vision and mission statements should be modified. Often, these sessions took many hours, even though the resulting statements ended up being quite short. Often, the more succinct the statement, the longer it takes to reach agreement. If your company follows a process like the ones I have described, then take the time to understand and even memorize those statements.

Most employees of companies, large or small, would be embarrassed if asked to recite (or even paraphrase) their company's vision and mission statements. Few take the time to memorize those important corporate statements.

But it's not entirely their fault; company leaders often fail to communicate, or even fail to develop, mission and vision statements to guide their operations. Even fewer will also develop a set of core values that articulate what the company holds dear with respect to corporate execution in pursuit of its long-term vision.

Research shows that the leaders in most American companies understand that they need to produce mission and vision statements to ensure that everyone in the organization is working toward a common goal. As Proverbs 21:5 says, "The plans of the diligent lead to profit."

However, many companies are not doing a good job of communicating these mission and vision statements—or inspiring their teams to understand, agree with, and internalize core values.

A 2016 Gallup poll revealed that just 23 percent of US employees strongly agree that they can *apply* their organization's values to their work every day. Only 27 percent strongly agree that they *believe in* their organization's values. The poll also revealed that there is a huge gap between many companies' desired culture and their actual culture. The authors of the study write, "The most successful companies that Gallup has studied don't see culture as a stand-alone initiative or program; instead, they take a comprehensive and integrated approach to creating and sustaining it. By approaching culture as a way to bring the company's purpose to life—and create a brand that uniquely meets customers' needs—these businesses…build a strategic foundation for outstanding performance."[32]

The Difference between a Vision Statement and a Mission Statement

It can be confusing to distinguish between a vision statement and a mission statement unless you understand the difference between the two. The Society for Human Resource Management explains the purpose of both statements:[33]

A *vision statement* looks forward and creates a mental image of the ideal state that the organization wishes to achieve. It is inspirational and aspirational and should challenge employees. A vision statement reveals answers to these questions:

- What problem are we seeking to solve?
- Where are we headed?
- If we achieved all our strategic goals, what would we look like ten years from now?

In contrast, a *mission statement* is a concise explanation of the organization's reason for existence—its *raison d'être*. It describes the company's purpose and overall intention. The mission statement supports the vision and communicates purpose and direction to employees, customers, vendors, and other stakeholders. The mission statement reveals answers to these questions:

- What is our organization's purpose?
- Why does our organization exist?

In other words, a vision statement focuses on the *future*, while a mission statement focuses on the *present*.

Not surprisingly, the most impactful mission and vision statements are brief and easy to understand. For a vision statement and mission statement to impact an organization's culture, reputation, and performance, every single person who works for the organization should be familiar with both statements and make key decisions that align well with those statements.

Here are examples of six of the most compelling vision and mission statements of a few of today's largest and most successful companies:[34]

Company Name	Mission Statement *(Why the Company Exists)*	Vision Statement *(Goal for the Future)*
Amazon	We strive to offer our customers the lowest possible prices, the best available selection, and the utmost convenience.	To be Earth's most customer-centric company, where customers can find and discover anything they might want to buy online.
Google	To organize the world's information and make it universally accessible and useful.	To provide access to the world's information in one click.
LinkedIn	To connect the world's professionals to make them more productive and successful.	To create economic opportunity for every member of the global workforce.

Company Name	Mission Statement (Why the Company Exists)	Vision Statement (Goal for the Future)
Southwest Airlines	Dedication to the highest quality of customer service delivered with a sense of warmth, friendliness, individual pride, and company spirit.	To become the world's most loved, most flown, and most profitable airline.
Tesla	To accelerate the world's transition to sustainable energy.	To create the most compelling car company of the 21st century by driving the world's transition to electric vehicles.
Uber	To bring transportation—for everyone, everywhere.	Smarter transportation with fewer cars and greater access. Transportation that's safer, cheaper, and more reliable; transportation that creates more job opportunities and higher incomes for drivers.

Why a Company's Vision and Mission Matter

Why are vision and mission statements important?

First, because even though companies *exist* to generate revenue or add to shareholder value, they will *thrive* by providing a deeper, more compelling solution to people's needs. Employees who are passionate about the company's mission often fall in love with their work, experience higher productivity levels and engagement, and express loyalty to the company. This can lead to longer tenures that ultimately can benefit the organization's bottom line over time.

A study by Imperative reveals that mission-driven workers are 54 percent more likely to stay for five years at a company and 30 percent more likely to grow into high performers than those who arrive at work with only their paycheck as the motivator.[35]

Second, companies that stand for something meaningful are much more likely to attract top talent.

In 2016, Millennials (born between 1981 and 1996) became the largest segment of the workforce.[36] This generation cares deeply about doing good in the world. In fact, 86 percent of Millennials said they would consider taking a pay cut to work at a company whose mission and values align with their own, according to LinkedIn's latest Workplace Culture report. By comparison, only 9 percent of Baby Boomers (those born between 1946 and 1964) would consider such a pay cut.[37]

These are attention-getting numbers! If you interview with, or join, a company that does not have a compelling mission and vision, you are far less likely to experience a fulfilling early vocational experience.

Prepare Well and Then Showcase
Your Knowledge during Interviews

My first piece of advice is, even before you accept that first full-time permanent position, when you are interviewing with companies, read, understand and prepare well for your interviews. During the interview process, mention and ask questions about the mission and vision.

In chapter 4, I recommend regularly asking the Holy Spirit for guidance in tough decision making. A perfect example of something you ought to pray over and seek the guidance of the Holy Spirit for is deciding whether or not to accept a new position with a new company. Ask for such guidance even before you have attended your first interview with the company.

As a result of your line of inquiry, if you find your own passions are well-aligned with their mission, let it be known. Demonstrating a passion for the company's mission is a compelling reason for them to make you an offer and for you to accept it.

Even before you begin employment, you will have impressed your potential new employer as someone who represents a good fit and who will embrace the corporate mission. In the interview process, you will have already enhanced your future career path.

Memorize the Statements

My next piece of advice is, if the company you have decided to work for has vision and mission statements, commit them to memory. You don't need to actually recite them; just memorize them so that they are embedded in your brain and you can instantly recall them.

With that knowledge and instant-recall ability, you will be well-equipped to assess decisions that your colleagues or superiors are making to determine if those decisions are consistent with the mission and vision. It is critically important for a company's actions to be consistent with its mission.

As a relatively new employee, if you observe actions that seem inconsistent with the corporate mission, I advise you not to overreact.

However, you could bring it up in a non-confrontational, non-threatening way with your own immediate supervisor. Early in your career, you don't want to appear to be challenging the wisdom of decisions made by superiors. But on the other hand, it is an opportunity to demonstrate your understanding of the company's mission and your commitment to the company's best interests. If you decide to communicate your concern, do it in the form of a question. For example, you might say, somewhat matter-of-factly, "I noticed the company's decision to [*state the decision*]. I may be missing something, but this appears to be inconsistent with our mission as a company. Am I wrong in making that observation?"

That's a soft approach to open a discussion, ostensibly for your own understanding. It is a very delicate question to be asking someone who may have been instrumental in the decision you are questioning and may possess a high level of ownership in it. So once again, this is a discussion that requires you to ask the Holy Spirit for guidance *before* you enter the conversation. The Holy Spirit will provide opportunities to do so and will also give you a nudge if you don't recognize the opportunity.

Later, maybe sooner than you realize, you will be making similar decisions that need to be tested for consistency with the corporate mission.

How You'll Benefit from Knowing These Statements

In my experience, few employees can even *paraphrase* their company's mission and vision statements, and it is the rare person indeed who can *recite* them. You will probably never be asked to recite these statements, and I don't recommend that you do so. That would likely be perceived as arrogant or presumptuous.

However, there are subtle ways in which it will become evident to others that you are aware of those important corporate statements. The implication will be that you share the company's passion.

You can fill in the blanks of the following examples of statements when communicating with your superiors and peers. When you do so, it will subtly convey your understanding and buy-in of these important company proclamations.

For example, when you learn about a new and exciting mission-driven project, you can say, "This initiative by the company makes so much sense in light of our mission to _____" or "This project is a brilliant way to accelerate our path to achieving our vision of _____."

By performing the simple act of memorizing the corporate mission and vision statements, and then demonstrating your awareness of them, you will certainly increase your visibility within the organization. You also will distinguish yourself as someone who has the potential to take on more responsibilities and rise through the ranks of the company.

CHAPTER 8

DEVELOP CULTURAL AND ORGANIZATIONAL AWARENESS

"Let the wise listen and add to their learning, and let the discerning get guidance."

—Proverbs 1:5

In any environment, it pays to be keenly aware of what's going on around you. This is certainly the case when you are navigating a new work environment. The more you observe how people interact with one another and how important projects and tasks get done, the better you will be able to shine in your professional role. However, even before accepting a new position, it is important to identify any inappropriate elements of the company's culture that may conflict with your own value system.

A Warning about Inappropriate Elements of Culture

In speaking about a company's culture, the verse below immediately comes to mind as a warning to Christians. As Paul admonished in 1 Corinthians 1:11–12, quarrels can exist and can cause division if it is not clear who should be followed. As a Christian, you must anchor yourself in following Christ. Anything in a corporate culture that seems at odds with your beliefs should be an indication that the company is not acting in concert with your own values.

"My brothers and sisters, some from Chloe's household have informed me that there are quarrels among you. What I mean is this: One of you says, 'I follow Paul'; another, 'I follow Apollos'; another, 'I follow Cephas'; still another, 'I follow Christ.'"
—1 Corinthians 1:11–12

I think specifically of a company that, a few years ago, was having a well-publicized Bacchanalia-like party with nudity and excessive drinking. The leadership considered those activities not only normal but a desired element of the culture. That might be an extreme example, but Christians should beware of such aspects of culture.

If you see elements of corporate culture that give you pause, avoid conformity, as Paul implores us to do in another passage in his letter to the Romans, chapter 12:

"Do not conform to the pattern of this world but be transformed by the renewing of your mind. Then you will be able to test and approve what God's will is—his good, pleasing and perfect will."
—Romans 12:2

With that as a warning, let me elaborate on the more typical and important elements of corporate culture that will help you to discern the ones you should embrace. Assume for the moment that you are seeing no red flags or objectionable elements in your company's culture.

Now, before you can be aware of your company's culture, let's look at what culture really is.

Culture Is an Organization's Identity

Much has been written about culture. It's a somewhat elusive concept because you can't measure it. In essence, it's the "vibe" of an organization. It's the atmosphere, the "feel" of a company.

Sometimes people think a company's culture is all about the perks it offers, but a culture is much more than that. Culture encompasses the values, mission, and vision of a company's leaders.

Natalie Baumgartner, PhD, is the Chief Workforce Scientist for an employee-engagement platform called Achievers. She defines *culture* as an organization's identity. She says it's important for a company's culture to be defined in a very simple and accessible way so everyone from the CEO all the way down to the junior-most employee can understand it. Baumgartner writes, "Culture is really the small set of values that determine how you do things in your organization on a daily basis. These values should drive the three main buckets of business behavior: how you communicate, what you prioritize, and what gets rewarded."[38]

Many Employees Value Culture over Compensation

Culture is so important that many job seekers—millennials in particular—value a strong company culture over higher pay. (Millennials were born between 1981 and 1996 and are between twenty-six and forty years old in 2020.)

In June 2019, Glassdoor, a global jobs website, conducted a survey among five thousand adults in the United States, the UK, France, and Germany. The study revealed that 56 percent of workers ranked a strong workplace culture as more important than salary, with more than three in four workers saying they would consider a company's culture before applying for a job there. In the United States, 65 percent of millennials valued company culture more than a high income, compared to 52 percent of Americans over the age of forty-five.[39]

Also, 73 percent of Glassdoor's respondents said they would not apply to a company unless its values aligned with their own. Two-thirds of employees said their firm's culture was one of the main reasons for staying in their jobs. And 74 percent of adults from the United States said they would look for a role elsewhere if their current company's culture deteriorated.[40]

A Positive Culture Helps Companies Retain Employees

When culture is well defined and appealing to prospective and current employees, that culture actually impacts the bottom line in a positive way.

Research shows that a company's culture has a direct impact on employee turnover, which affects productivity and therefore success.

According to *Business News Daily*, "Worker retention is as much a problem of culture as it is of compensation. If your business is experiencing high turnover, analyze your business culture and consider the opportunities you can provide employees for career growth and development...Building a better business culture is key to keeping employees engaged. By increasing engagement, you can drive worker retention. A Gallup study found that employees who are engaged at work are 59 percent less likely to look for a different job in the next 12 months...Building a better business culture doesn't mean providing employee perks, like ping pong tables. It means recruiting workers who fit your organization's vision and providing employees with autonomy.[41]

A Company's Culture Promotes Some Behaviors and Inhibits Others

Although every organization's culture is unique, some researchers have attempted to categorize various types of culture.

For example, according to Robert E. Quinn and Kim S. Cameron at the University of Michigan at Ann Arbor, there are four types of organizational culture: Clan, Adhocracy, Market, and Hierarchy. Here is how they describe the four types of culture:[42]

- Clan-oriented cultures are family-like, with a focus on mentoring, nurturing, and "doing things together."
- Adhocracy-oriented cultures are dynamic and entrepreneurial, with a focus on risk-taking, innovation, and "doing things first."
- Market-oriented cultures are results-oriented, with a focus on competition, achievement, and "getting the job done."
- Hierarchy-oriented cultures are structured and controlled, with a focus on efficiency, stability, and "doing things right."

Quinn and Cameron believe that all cultures promote some forms of behavior and inhibit others. For example, they associate the Hierarchy and Market cultures with a principal focus on stability, and they associate the Clan and Adhocracy cultures with flexibility and adaptability. A Hierarchy culture based on control will lead mainly to incremental change, while a focus on Adhocracy will more typically lead to breakthrough change. But overall, they say the right culture will be one that closely fits the direction and strategy of a particular organization as it confronts its own issues and the challenges of a particular time.[43]

While this identification of the four types of organizational cultures may be difficult to discern as a new employee in a company, it is worthwhile for you to be aware of these variations as you go through your own discernment process. Ultimately, your objective in considering corporate culture is first to make sure you don't see anything inconsistent with your values and beliefs, and once you are beyond that test, then to determine how things get done at the company. Is there collaboration across departments, as might be the case in a Clan-oriented or Market-oriented culture? Or are the required tasks tightly structured from the top down, as might be the case in a Hierarchy-oriented culture?

Discerning Key Elements of Your Company's Culture and Organizational Structure

"An intelligent heart acquires knowledge, and the ear of the wise seeks knowledge."
—Proverbs 18:15

Every company has a unique culture. The more aware you are of the culture in your organization, the more easily you will be able to understand it, navigate it, and contribute to it. It takes some level of immersion into the organization and curiosity to acquire this knowledge.

One way to discover your company's culture and how things get accomplished is by networking throughout the company, with people at all different levels of the corporate hierarchy. The knowledge you gain about your organization and its culture will greatly facilitate your transition to increased responsibility.

The best way to start down this path is informally, such as in meetings, on lunch breaks, or after work with colleagues in other departments.

As you build your network throughout the organization, ask the following questions of colleagues in your own department and those in other departments. Keep a record of the things you have heard and learned in the process. It always helps as a memory facilitation device to capture, in writing, what you have learned.

Asking any of these questions will lead to other follow-up questions that will result in a far more enlightened knowledge of exactly how things get accomplished, especially within a large and diverse workforce. Here is a process and a line of inquiry you can follow:

1. For each person in your expanding network, determine their role and place within the organizational structure.
2. Ask how each person contributes to the mission of the organization.
3. Ask about their recent successes and also about any frustrations they have experienced.
4. Ask about projects they have worked on (or are now working on) that have required interfacing with other departments.
5. If multiple departments take part in major projects, ask how that effort is coordinated, who has authority to make decisions, and if there are any matrix-reporting situations (i.e. situations in which an employee has a split reporting relationship to more than one boss).
6. Ask if the company has a formal process for bringing forth innovative or creative new ideas (sometimes referred to as *ideation*). As you learn more about the culture and how things get accomplished, ideation can be a great way for you to gain recognition and visibility within your department and beyond.
7. Ask for candid views from those in your network on how the process is working and in what ways they believe the process could be improved.

As you interface with those in your network, remember the advice given in chapter 7 to consider ways in which you can offer your assistance to others outside your own departmental contacts.

For several years as president of New York Life, I arranged monthly breakfast meetings with six or seven employees from different departments, most of whom didn't know each other. At those meetings, I talked about the company's recent successes and strategies and then asked each person to speak about the questions numbered 1 and 2 above. It was an engaging activity, and the feedback I received from those sessions was remarkably strong. Most attendees indicated that they had learned a lot they hadn't known about the company and about their colleagues. In many cases, long-term, highly productive cross-departmental relationships developed.

I am strongly suggesting in this chapter that you take proactive efforts to build your network of contacts and come to understand your company's culture and gain awareness of its organizational structure.

Learning the nature of your company's culture and how things get done can be an important prerequisite for understanding the company's strategies and for developing your own strategic thinking capability, which we discuss in the next chapter.

CHAPTER 9

DEVELOP AND DEMONSTRATE STRATEGIC THINKING CAPABILITY

"Do you not know that in a race all the runners run, but only one gets the prize? Run in such a way as to get the prize."
—1 Corinthians 9:24

According to the *Business Dictionary, strategic thinking* is "the ability to come up with effective plans in line with an organization's objectives within a particular economic situation. Strategic thinking helps business managers review policy issues, perform long-term planning, set goals, determine priorities, and identify potential risks and opportunities."

If you can develop and demonstrate strategic thinking capability, you will stand out—not only among new and young employees, but even among more seasoned and long-tenured employees. In my corporate experience, even many senior officers of large companies simply didn't understand the difference between strategy and tactics.

Some people believe strategic thinking is an inherent talent that individuals either possess or don't. They think there is little way to develop such capability if you don't already possess the "gift." Even though (in chapter 1) I identified strategic leadership as one of my spiritual gifts, I believe that anyone can develop a strategic-thinking capability using the advice provided in this chapter, In fact, my own strategic capabilities were enhanced greatly through the effective mentoring of my own superiors, who were highly strategic in their thoughts and actions.

Let's look at what *strategy* means, its wartime origins, and its significance in business.

"Strategy" Applied to War Long before We Used It in Business

So, what is *strategy*, exactly?

The word "strategy" was originally used as a war term in determining the means by which a combatant would defeat the enemy. The Greek equivalent, *strategos*, means "general" or "army leader."

The concept of strategy dates back to biblical times and then to ancient China, when strategist and philosopher Sun Tzu offered thoughts on strategy that business and military leaders continue to study today. Sun Tzu's best-known work is *The Art of War*, a book in which he emphasized the creative and deceptive aspects of strategy. One of Sun Tzu's ideas that has numerous business applications is that winning a battle without fighting is the best way to win.[44]

In the early twentieth century, automobile maker Henry Ford emerged as one of the pioneers of strategic management among industrial leaders. At the time, cars seemed to be a luxury item for wealthy people. Ford adopted a unique strategic perspective, boldly offering the vision that he would make cars the average family could afford.[45]

In 1912, Harvard University became the first higher-education institution to offer a course focused on how business executives could lead their organizations to greater success.[46] Other universities followed suit, and before long, the wartime concept of strategy had been modified to apply to business.

In general, strategy as it relates to business is how to beat the competition in a way that creates and achieves sustainable competitive advantage.

Of course, in 1 Corinthians 9:24, Paul was not speaking about beating the competition in business, nor was he speaking literally about winning a race. He was speaking metaphorically about worshipping just one God and finding salvation and eternity as the first-place prize. Apply that same intensity and drive to developing corporate strategy. Remember that Jesus is your workplace partner, and He will help you achieve your lofty business objectives.

The Difference between Strategy and Tactics

Many employees—and some managers and leaders—don't understand the difference between *strategy* and *tactics*.

Strategy is how to leverage a company's core competencies to achieve its objectives and create sustainable competitive advantage. *Tactics* describe the specific actions that will be taken along the way.

According to the Strategic Thinking Institute, in the military realm, *tactics* teach the use of armed forces in engagements, while *strategy* teaches the use of engagements to achieve the goals of the war. The original meaning of tactics is "order"—the ordering of formations on the battlefield.[47]

Many people incorrectly think the difference between strategy and tactics is that strategy is long-term, and tactics are short-term. But both strategy and tactics can be either short-term or long-term.

Strategy is our path or bridge for going from where we are today to our goal. It's our general resource allocation plan. For example, one strategy might be to engage industry thought leaders to become advocates for our product. The related *tactics* are how we will specifically or tangibly do that. They might include direct-marketing letters, face-to-face meetings, key talking point scripts, and an iPad app. In general, if you can reach out and physically touch it, it's a tactic.[48]

Tips for Learning Your Company's Strategies

"The one who gets wisdom loves life; the one who cherishes understanding will soon prosper."
—Proverbs 19:8

The first step in your learning process is to understand your own company's strategies. Here are some easy ways to do that.

1. **Read your company's annual report, and ask for copies of the most recent strategic plan.** The company's annual report tends to be a promotional marketing report about the company's mission and recent successes. It typically touches only generally on the corporate mission and strategies. The strategic plan is more likely to be an internal report with an in-depth analysis of the company's strengths, weaknesses, opportunities, and threats. Following the SWOT analysis, you are likely to read more in the plan document about the competition and the specific strategies your company will deploy to create sustainable competitive advantage to beat the competition and increase market share.

2. **If your company has publicly traded stock, read the periodic reports of the analysts who follow that stock.** There you can

learn a lot more about the external view of your company's risks and opportunities and how it fares against the competition. You can also view reports of the various rating agencies, such as Moody's, S&P, or Fitch, that might be rating your company for creditworthiness or other purposes.

3. **Search for recent articles and press releases.** These documents, often available online, can uncover important recent actions of a company in the way of mergers, acquisitions, partnerships, and other potential strategic actions.

By the way, it will be beneficial to do as much of this research as possible even *before* your interview with a prospective employer.

Over the course of my career, I have interviewed dozens of candidates for employment. I can remember only a handful who did extensive pre-interview due diligence of this nature; it was very impressive and noticeable. Needless to say, I usually hired those who had taken the time and effort to study the company before arriving for their first interview.

Learn about Your Company's Competition

After gaining a far better understanding of your own company, then embark on a similar effort to understand the competition. Follow the same steps you used to research your company to research five or more key competitors.

There is a term for this; it's called *competitive intelligence*, or CI, and it simply means gathering data about competing companies in an ethical way.

You might have to ask the sales, marketing, or planning departments within your company who the key competitors are. If your company is a large company, key competitors might differ by business unit and/or product line. This task might be more difficult than researching your own company, but I assure you, it will be well worth your time and effort.

Here are some tips for gathering CI on your competitors:

1. **Read as much publicly available material as you can.** Try to get your hands on their strategic plans for the future. For large or expensive products (like automobiles or appliances) at a minimum, you should be able to understand companies' product differentiation by reading product manuals, marketing pieces, and press releases. A LexisNexis search can reveal important news and legal proceedings.

2. **Mystery-shop the competition.** If you really want to take your due diligence up a notch, and your business is in retail product sales, purchase some of the competitor's products to compare them against comparable products sold by your company. Determine what they are doing to gain an edge over your company. Call and/or visit their offices or stores, subscribe to blogs, and get on their mailing lists to find out how their customer service, support, sales, follow-up, marketing, and other business practices compare with those of your company. And don't forget to take notes. If you don't take notes and you are studying multiple competitors, you will begin to confuse one with another.

3. **Set up a Google alert on your own company and on its competitors.** You will discover what's being said and reported about all the companies. You can find instructions for setting up a Google alert at https://support.google.com/websearch/answer/4815696?hl=en.

4. **Get acquainted with your company's distributors.** They are out in the field, talking with your customers. They are likely to hear opinions about your competitors' products and services—

specifically about features your competitors offer that your company does not. Ask if there are some aspects of your business offerings that they would like to see expanded or modified. Ask the same questions on social media. Also, try to understand why your customers prefer your company over others.

5. **Review competing companies' websites.** You can learn a great deal by exploring key competitors' websites. You are likely to find their mission statements, product offerings, and how customers can access information or even make purchases online.

How to Convert This Knowledge into Strategic Thinking Capability

The title of this chapter suggests that a person has to *develop and demonstrate* strategic thinking capability. If you do everything above, you will have a far better understanding of what strategy is and how it applies to your company and its competitors.

So how can you convert this knowledge into strategic thinking capabilities that your peers and superiors will notice. Knowing what your company and its competitors do (or are planning to do) to beat each other is wonderful, but it won't necessarily demonstrate strategic thinking capability.

Once you have gained valuable knowledge by completing the steps just mentioned, thoughtfully consider the following questions. The answers to these questions will lead you to demonstrate a strong strategic thinking capability:

1. How does my company currently differentiate itself from its key competitors?

2. What do we do differently and/or better than anybody else? Can we build on that, and if so, how?

3. What unique products, product features or benefits does my company have that others don't have? Are there others we should be considering?

4. Are there consumer needs or desires that my company and/or its competitors are not currently meeting? What are ways we can meet those needs?

5. How does my company compare to its competitors in customer surveys relating to products or services? If we fall short in some areas, what types of cost-effective investments can we make to significantly improve in those areas?

6. How does our advertising, marketing, and branding stack up against the competition? How can we improve in this regard?

7. Are there market segments that our competition is not adequately penetrating that we can effectively expand into?

8. From a competitive employment perspective, how do our compensation and benefits compare to those of our key competitors? To what extent do we need to step up our own compensation and benefit packages to better compete for talent?

If you have done your homework, asking yourself these questions and then answering them should trigger many strategic ideas that will help your company create sustainable competitive advantage. A thoughtful exercise like this is highly strategic and the answers you come up with could lead to potentially new and expanded strategies for your company.

As you communicate your thoughts and ideas to your company's management team, the outcome will be their awareness and recognition of you as a highly strategic thinker with high potential for more senior roles in the organization. However, once again, I caution you to ask the Holy Spirit for guidance. Rather than proactively raising such issues on your own with your management, rely on the Holy Spirit to create those opportunities for you and also to nudge you if you are not recognizing them.

CHAPTER 10

UNDERSTAND THE FINANCIAL UNDERPINNINGS OF THE BUSINESS

"Listen to advice and accept discipline, and at the end you will be counted among the wise."
—Proverbs 19:20

"I will instruct you and teach you in the way you should go; I will counsel you with my loving eye on you."
—Psalm 32:8

In all aspects of building a fulfilling Christ-centered career, including the important step of understanding your company's financial underpinnings be mindful of the wisdom of the Old Testament as expressed in the above verses from Proverbs and Psalms. They apply to many aspects of what I am suggesting in this chapter.

Ask the Lord to open your mind to a better understanding of the financial results. Then listen for His instruction and advice as communicated to you through the Holy Spirit and facilitated by knowledgeable colleagues at the company.

As I read in my daily devotionals, from the books of Psalms and Proverbs, I am reminded of, and amazed by, their wisdom and applicability today. In the New Testament, Jesus Himself alludes to the importance of planning and understanding the financial consequences of our personal or business decisions in the following passage from the Gospel of Luke:

> *"Suppose one of you wants to build a tower. Won't you first sit down and estimate the cost to see if you have enough money to complete it? For if you lay the foundation and are not able to finish it, everyone who sees it will ridicule you, saying, 'This person began to build and wasn't able to finish.'"*
>
> —Luke 14:28–30

After the advice in chapters 1 through 5 on applying biblical principles in the workplace, and chapter 15 on "Balancing Faith, Family, and Career," I consider the advice in this chapter the next most important in the book. Following this advice has substantially elevated the visibility and recognition of hundreds of people who have heard my presentations on the topic.

The Biggest Career Blocker

As the president of New York Life Insurance Company, I saw many young people, and even high-level executives, place self-imposed limits on their advancement because they paid little or no attention to their companies' financial results. Nor did they appropriately consider the financial impact of their decisions.

Later, as I thought about my New York Life experience, I asked myself, "What is the biggest career blocker and deficiency among employees at all levels?"

The answer came to me quickly: they simply don't understand or appreciate the importance of financial results. Too often, people focus solely on top-line sales and revenue growth, almost to the exclusion of balancing a budget and achieving a strong bottom line or profit. Even worse, too many executives can't even read a financial statement, much less manage to one.

Financial acumen might not be one of your spiritual gifts as identified in the exercise in chapter 1 of this book. Not everyone possesses that skill. As a result, understanding financial statements comes easy for some, but for many others, it is intimidating and confusing.

If you have never taken an accounting or a business course, don't despair. What I am about to propose is something that requires no such background. It's a challenge that I hope you'll embrace enthusiastically because at the end of day, you will get noticed and likely will be labeled a high-potential employee. Pray for guidance in understanding the concepts well enough to apply the knowledge to your specific role, in the ways I describe below.

Focus on Top-Line and Bottom-Line Growth Simultaneously

The term "top-line" typically refers to a company's revenues, which are largely generated by sales of the company's products and services for the accounting period. The term "bottom line" refers to the company's net profits for the same accounting period.

In my experience as a president of a Fortune 100 company and as a director of several for-profit corporations, I have observed that most executives aspire to run a business. They often say, "I want to manage a P&L" (profit-and-loss statement). They even vigorously campaign for such opportunities within their organizations.

The primary reason many never get the opportunity (or worse, fail when they do get the opportunity) is that they don't recognize this simple fact: the key to success in business and in career advancement is not in achieving strong top-line growth or strong bottom-line growth, but rather in *accomplishing both simultaneously*. This is equally true whether you are working for a large public corporation, for a small business, or in a burgeoning entrepreneurial venture.

In many businesses, it's easy to achieve impressive top-line growth if you're not concerned with the bottom line. Just undercut the competition in pricing and overpay distributors. Doing so can produce dramatic sales growth, but at the expense of the bottom line. That's not a sustainable proposition.

Conversely, it is relatively easy in the short run to achieve strong bottom-line growth if you're not concerned about top-line growth. Just cut costs significantly while underpaying and overworking your employees and ignoring the quality of customer service. Such a strategy almost always leads to business failures, despite short-term bottom-line profits.

I have encountered top executives who were making seven-figure incomes who couldn't successfully run a business. Why? Because they focused almost exclusively on top-line revenue growth but either ignored, or didn't understand, the bottom-line profit impacts of their decisions.

A Remarkable American Business Success Story

The best example I have of a successful business that fully embraced this concept was that of the pharmaceutical benefit manager Express Scripts. The New York Life Insurance Company purchased Express Scripts for a few million dollars in 1989, and I served on the company's board for several years.

In the subsequent twenty-five years, the company grew dramatically. After going public in 1992 and before being acquired by Cigna in 2018, its market capitalization (i.e., the aggregate value of its outstanding shares) had grown to more than $50 billion, and Express Scripts was among the top twenty-five Fortune 500 companies.

When asked about the company's high-level financial objectives, Barrett Toan (the company's CEO during many years of rapid growth) would simply articulate his elevator speech, which was, "Thirty percent top-line growth and thirty percent bottom-line growth every year." The company actually achieved that feat year after year, and that fueled the significant growth in its market value and high ranking among the Fortune 500 companies.

A Proven Strategy—And the Killer Question

If you do not understand your company's balance sheet and income statement, don't worry—you don't need to pursue an MBA in finance or take a series of courses in accounting. Even someone who has no such educational background can gain a rudimentary knowledge of the key elements of both the balance sheet and the income statement.

Simply seek out someone from the Finance or Accounting Department at your company who is willing to spend a little time with you to provide a high-level understanding of the financial reports. You don't need to understand how all the detailed accounting entries are recorded, or even what every line item in the full income statement or balance sheet means. It's sufficient to know how the income statement is constructed and how it flows into the balance sheet during each accounting period. In a few short meetings, you most certainly will be able to become familiar with the essential elements of the financial statements of your company.

Once you have developed that rudimentary knowledge, here's a two-part strategy that will distinguish you from most other employees—and even from many senior officers in the company:

1. Develop a spreadsheet that tracks (on a quarterly basis) the three highest-level summary numbers from the income statement (Revenues, Expenses, and Net Profit/Loss) and three from the balance sheet (Assets, Liabilities, and Net Equity). If you just do that much and watch the changes from quarter to quarter, you will probably be in a small minority of employees who are familiar with those results and how they are changing over time.

   Updating that sheet with six new numbers every quarter won't take you more than a minute or two, but it might be the best investment of time you'll ever make in your career.

2. Once you gain comfort and confidence with the quarterly results, expand your understanding by going back to the person in Accounting to ask the killer question: "What drives the profitability of our business?"

   You will probably shock your contact in the Accounting Department. My bet is, the initial answer will be something like, "I'll have to get back to you on that."

Later, you can expand your knowledge into a more granular understanding by asking for breakouts of the key drivers, by business unit. As you advance in the organization, it will become even more important for you to fully understand the drivers of future profitable growth. Identify and track these drivers early in your tenure at the company, and then continue to monitor them while your career flourishes.

As your knowledge increases and as your friend in the Accounting Department continues to answer future questions and enhance your business development, I wouldn't be surprised if the CEO of your company, even if it's a large company, will hear that you were asking such questions. I have great confidence in my statement that the CEO will hear about you because many young graduates have told me that it happened to them when they followed this simple advice.

As you advance in your career, don't lose sight of the fact that every decision you make should be informed by its financial implications. Go back often to the important drivers identified in the answers to *the killer question*!

Also, never forget the advice in chapters 1 through 5 on biblical principles in the workplace. In addition to being informed by financial implications, your decisions must be consistent with your values and beliefs, they must be mindful of the Golden Rule, and they must be decisions and actions your workplace partner—Jesus—would find pleasing.

CHAPTER 11

TAKE CHARGE OF YOUR OWN DEVELOPMENT

"Lazy hands make for poverty, but diligent hands bring wealth."
—Proverbs 10:4

In a sense, this entire book is about self-development. Some aspects of self-development are covered in other chapters—for example, The Golden Rule in chapter 5; preparing for meetings in chapter 12; presentation skills in chapter 13; and balancing faith, family, and career in chapter 15.

Recent trends suggest that pressure on corporate profits has led to sometimes extreme expense controls. Controlling expenses too aggressively not only stresses out the workforce; it also can result in companies limiting their expenditures on training and development for their employees.

No matter what your position is within your company, don't assume that your superiors will closely monitor, take a strong interest in, or offer to contribute to your development. You might need to take charge of your own professional development, even if it means using some of your evenings, weekends, or vacation time to participate in developmental activities.

This chapter suggests many ways in which employees can self-educate. Don't be scared away by the extensiveness of these recommendations. Of all the chapters in this book, the advice in this one can and should be staged over time. Much of it will be most relevant after you have been on the job for a couple of years or longer. Over time, you can come back to the book (or the supplemental workbook) periodically and review this chapter for ongoing developmental advice.

The list of suggestions is long and includes many strategies I followed during my career, but certainly not within my first year or two of employment. If you attempt to develop your skills too quickly, you risk burning out—or worse, sacrificing the attentiveness you need to give to your primary job responsibilities.

Nonetheless, it is extremely important to be aware of areas in which you need development and to articulate a plan to address them. Your plan should indicate an expected timetable for these pursuits. You will need to review and revise your initial plan often because your work situation will most likely change, and you might need to modify it accordingly.

There is no cookie-cutter approach to development because it needs to be customized for your own work situation and specific needs. But, in general, here are the most important steps to take in your own self-development:

1. Create a vision of where you want to be in five years.
2. Develop a plan to achieve the necessary skills to help you get there.

3. Track your progress against the plan.
4. Review the plan regularly, and revise it as needed.

My Own Development Experience

I started my insurance career as an actuarial student at John Hancock Mutual Life Insurance Company in Boston. As an actuarial student, I was expected to achieve professional designations, which required passing an extremely difficult series of nine professional examinations. Even though I was paid a salary, my primary day-to-day responsibility was to study for those exams while taking on occasional projects. For almost three years, I didn't even know who my boss was, and I was rarely given any meaningful assignments. For some extended periods, I had no work assignments at all.

I was forced to find my own work and to take steps to develop myself. As it turns out, that was one of the best things that ever happened to me. It got me started down a path of self-development that led to much more gratification and success than if I had simply sat back and tried to enjoy being paid to do almost nothing, other than study for the exams.

I will share with you the kinds of things I found useful in my self-development, not only early in my career, but throughout my career.

Development Tips in Four Broad Categories

In this chapter, I have identified some development tips in broad categories. You may already be proficient in some of these areas, so try to identify those that will aid you the most in achieving your vision. Build your plan with a timetable around those areas of greatest and most urgent need.

Here are the four categories:

1. Adjust your mind-set.
2. Increase your productivity.

3. Remain current in your field of expertise.
4. Hone your people skills.

Let's look at each one of these categories in detail.

1. Adjust Your Mind-Set

"Do not conform to the pattern of this world, but be transformed by the renewing of your mind."
—Romans 12:2

A. Develop a Growth Mentality

Recognize that you will either stagnate at your current level, or you will accept the challenge and effort required to grow and develop. Commit to doing what it takes to enable your own professional growth.

Recognize that this will be a lifelong learning process, and view minor setbacks as learning experiences, as opposed to failures. I always learned from my mistakes, and I believe I developed more rapidly as a result of those mistakes. Don't be afraid to take risks, accept difficult challenges, and even make some mistakes.

B. Define Your Success Based on Your beliefs and Values

In chapter 2, you went through the exercise of identifying your core beliefs and values. With those in mind, it will be much easier for you to determine what truly makes you happy and how you will get there. And this will greatly facilitate the establishment of your future development plan. Identify what you believe will define success for you professionally in five years.

C. Be Willing to take on new challenges

Much of your development will involve your existing areas of expertise and job responsibilities and may be somewhat limited to your own close circle of associates. But be prepared to step out of your comfort zone, particularly if you are asked to serve on an interdepartmental project or task force.

Such an assignment might seem risky or difficult, but the upside is that you will meet new colleagues, expand your network, and probably gain a better understanding of how things work at the company. I always welcomed and even sought such opportunities.

D. Take Initiative on Your Own Behalf

Be proactive in taking the initiative to make your professional growth a priority. Don't hesitate to periodically ask your supervisor or manager for the following:

- Feedback on how you're doing
- How you can improve
- Steps he or she thinks you can take to grow and develop

To avoid coming across as though you are concerned only about your own personal development, find a way to tie these topics in with the company's vision and mission. For example, you could ask, "How do you think I am doing in terms of executing my responsibilities in a way that contributes to the company's mission and vision?"

This does not have to wait for an annual performance review, ask these questions at least annually. Be sure to phrase the questions in a way that indicates your desire to better support the mission and vision of the company. Then work hard to demonstrate your commitment to making those improvements.

2. Increase Your Productivity

"Whatever you do, work at it with all your heart, as working for the Lord, not for human masters, since you know that you will

receive an inheritance from the Lord as a reward. It is the Lord Christ you are serving."
—Colossians 3:23–24

A. Improve Your Time Management

If you already feel overworked (and my guess is, you do), then it might seem impossible to dedicate time to self-development. Delegating tasks to others is one effective way to deal with this, but you might not currently be in a management role that allows you to delegate.

As mentioned in chapter 6, one obvious way to improve productivity while demonstrating your commitment to the company is to spend more time in the office. However, that is not what I have in mind regarding a way to improve your time management. If you are honest with yourself, you might have more down time than you realize. You might be dealing with personal matters during working hours, and you might not be addressing the most important tasks with the priority they deserve.

According to a web survey by America Online and Salary.com, the average worker admits to frittering away 2.09 hours per day, not counting lunch. Over the course of a year (and even after accounting for time that employers expect to be wasted), that adds up to $759 billion in salaries—in the United States only—for which companies receive no apparent benefit. Nearly 45 percent of the 10,044 employee respondents indicated that the number one way they waste time at work is personal internet use (email, IM, online polls, interactive games, message boards, chat rooms, etc.). Socializing with coworkers was the second most prevalent form of wasting time at work (23.4 percent of respondents). Conducting personal business, "spacing out," running errands, and making personal phone calls were other prevalent workplace time-wasting activities.[49]

Managers don't expect you to work at your full capacity all the time; however, most will notice when people are slacking off. To fast-start your career, be known as one of the team members who is highly productive.

B. Prioritize

Whether or not you are able to delegate, prioritize your assignments. Focus on those that are most important, while eliminating or deferring others that are less important.

Throughout your career, you'll be confronted with competing tasks that require your attention. As your workload increases, it might seem impossible to accomplish everything. I often said to my employees, "We can do anything, but we can't do everything."

What I have observed over and over again in businesses is how difficult it is to stop doing something that has always been done in the past, even if it is totally unnecessary. There are many approaches to improving efficiency. A few examples are to use productivity tools such as apps and software and to redesign processes.

When your work is piling up and there's not enough time to do it all, it's easy to feel overwhelmed. One simple way to tame your growing list of priorities is to write them all down or type them into your computer or phone. Then rank them according to their urgency and importance. If someone is expecting a project by a certain time, that has to come first. If you have a project that will take only an hour to finish and another will take an entire day, finish the shorter project first. Large-scale projects can seem overwhelming if you try to finish them all at once. Break them down into manageable chunks, and finish some of the work each day.

Tim Elmore, president of a nonprofit leadership training and development organization, suggests asking yourself the following three questions to help you determine your highest priorities:[50]

1. **What is required of me in this role?** Identify tasks and objectives that are necessary parts of your job.
2. **What produces the greatest results when I do it?** List the activities you do that result in the most "fruit"—activities that people agree you're very good at.
3. **What is most fulfilling when I do it?** As you reflect on your projects and tasks, note the ones that are deeply satisfying—the ones you love and would enjoy even if you weren't paid to do them.

C. Maintain a "To-Do" List

I know it might sound old-fashioned, but I have always relied heavily on daily to-do lists to help me prioritize projects and allocate my time. Listing all assignments in writing also has allowed me to determine the priority I should give to each task. There are many software packages and apps on the market that can help you set up your to-do list format.

You will be surprised at how much more you can accomplish. You will derive a lot of satisfaction from watching your productivity improve as you update your daily list and realize how many things you are accomplishing.

To ground myself in what's most important and to help me set priorities, every Friday evening, I would identify the top few tasks that I felt must be done in the following week. You'll find that this brings a sense of closure to the current week and sets you up for a running start to the subsequent week. This simple practice will also enhance your enjoyment of the weekend and your ability to get good nights' rest over the weekend.

Whether you jot down your to-do list in a notebook or type it on your computer or phone, the simple act of making the list can be motivating. Dr. Tim Pychyl, an expert in the area of procrastination research, says you will feel an immediate sense of accomplishment simply by writing down all the tasks you would like to complete, without completing any one of them. This is because your brain will simulate the success you would like to feel.[51]

Some experts warn against writing vague, one-word tasks on your to-do list. The tasks should be specific. David Allen, who is considered a to-do-list guru, suggests **writing your task down as actions**. This will prevent you from using nonspecific terms when making your list. For example, instead of writing "Start and finish research for Tim," word the first task necessary for that project as, "Do a journal article search using the terms XYZ." Every time you write down a new to-do, Allen suggests asking yourself, "What is step number one to get this task done?" Step number one becomes your new to-do.[52]

3. Remain Current in Your Field of Expertise

"A wise man is full of strength, and a man of knowledge enhances his might."
—Proverbs 24:5 (ESV)

A. Seek Out Educational Experiences

For your particular job responsibilities, or areas of expertise, consider attending seminars or conferences and/or getting certificates, designations, or degrees, if they are available. If fees are involved, many companies will pay for such development activities. They might not suggest them for you, however; you might need to ask about particular programs you would like to attend.

Do a little research into what programs would be most effective for you, given your job responsibilities and the state of your current knowledge. Maintaining up-to-date professional skills in a rapidly changing environment will be critical to your long-term success.

B. Bring Back Actionable Ideas from Your Training

When you attend seminars or educational programs, always be thinking about the three or four key takeaways you can implement to benefit you and your company.

I had bosses who told me I was extremely effective in extracting meaningful information that led to significant improvements at my company every single time I attended a meeting or conference. If you develop that kind of reputation, you'll have no trouble getting approval for participation in other such programs, even when an added expense is required.

C. Participate in Professional Organizations

Some of the best developmental experiences of my career were a result of my volunteer participation in industry associations and in involvement with task forces or important committees. The enormous benefits included the following:

- A greatly expanded network of industry contacts
- The sharing of best practices in my field
- Maintaining current knowledge of changes in legislation and regulations that could affect my profession and/or my company
- The ability to better understand the competition and their strategies
- Early recognition of emerging trends in the business

This is a suggestion that will require a commitment of your time. As a result, I recommend that you consider it after at least a couple of years on the job.

Don't make the mistake of assuming that you need to be expert in your field to join such task forces, committees, or advisory boards. On the contrary, organizers are constantly looking for more participants. Getting involved will actually accelerate your ability to become a recognized expert. It will also lead to your being well-connected, which is always valuable in a business setting.

4. Hone Your People Skills

"Therefore encourage one another and build each other up, just as in fact you are doing."
—1 Thessalonians 5:11

A. Expand Your Internal Network

Make an effort to meet other employees at all levels within your organization and across multiple departments. Be inquisitive about what they do, what kinds of projects they are working on, and how they support the mission of the company.

As you learn more about them and their work, think about ways in which you might be able to help them out. Of course, you must give priority attention to your own job responsibilities first, but learning about other areas within the organization will give you a well-rounded business experience.

B. Get to Know Your Colleagues

Take an interest in the work history, careers, goals, and aspirations of the fellow workers you meet. Ask them about their families and the aspects of their jobs that give them personal gratification. Make a conscious effort not to spend a lot of time talking about yourself until you are asked. I say "make a conscious effort" because so many of us instinctively want to tell other people about ourselves. I'm sure you can immediately recall people who incessantly talk about themselves and their accomplishments and never ask you a single question. Don't fall into that trap.

C. Listen Intently

"My dear brothers and sisters, take note of this: Everyone should be quick to listen, slow to speak and slow to become angry."
—James 1:19

You probably won't be considered a great communicator unless you develop the ability to listen intently. I have had people tell me they thought we had a great conversation after I had said almost nothing. Often, I demonstrated assurances, and at times sympathy or empathy, almost entirely through body language.

On the other hand, I can think of several examples of behaviors I regretted when I interrupted someone or blurted out a response before allowing the other person the time to complete his or her point or argument. When you know someone really well, you often anticipate what they are going to say and react before they have had a chance to complete their comments. This is true at work, and it's true when we get into an argument with a spouse before we hear him or her out.

Winston Churchill said, "Courage is what it takes to stand up and speak; courage is also what it takes to sit down and listen." Listening well will add greatly to your own knowledge, and it will show that you truly respect and value what others are saying.

D. Develop Emotional Intelligence

Emotional intelligence, sometimes abbreviated as EQ, describes your control over your emotions and your level of empathy. Developing this skill can make you a better communicator. In addition, it can help you resolve workplace conflicts—a useful trait for leaders and managers, as well as other employees.

Decades of research now point to emotional intelligence as being the critical factor that sets star performers apart from the rest of the pack. The connection is so strong that 90 percent of top performers have high emotional intelligence. This intangible quality affects how we manage behavior, navigate social complexities, and make personal decisions to achieve positive results.[53]

Here are just some of the hallmarks of emotional intelligence. Work on strengthening these characteristics to increase your own EQ:

- You are curious about people.
- You embrace change.
- You know your strengths and weaknesses.
- You know how to say no to yourself and others.
- You let go of mistakes.
- You give without expecting anything in return.
- You appreciate what you have.

The many suggestions in this chapter for taking charge of your own self-development will greatly enhance your career. While many of your peers are waiting for their supervisors, the HR department, or someone else to suggest ways they can develop their skills, you will be proactively taking charge of your own development, thus turbo-charging your path to success.

CHAPTER 12
OVERPREPARE FOR EVERY MEETING

*"And let us consider how we may spur one another on toward love
and good deeds, not giving up meeting together, as some are in the
habit of doing, but encouraging one another—and all the more as
you see the Day approaching."*
—Hebrews 10:24–25

Inevitably, new employees are invited to attend meetings and at times
are asked to perform menial tasks like taking notes. Regardless of why
you are in attendance and what you are expected to do (even if the
expectation is to sit quietly and listen), take the time to overprepare.

As a new employee, you might feel hesitant about speaking up
during a meeting. That might be the right instinct, but depending on
the culture in your company, your comments might be welcome. Follow

the tips in this chapter to prepare for meetings and to feel far more comfortable in participating in the discussions.

Many Employees Are Afraid to Speak Up at Work

Being afraid to speak up is a common issue, even among employees who have been in their positions for a while. But staying silent about important issues can be costly to companies.

A 2018 report by leadership training company VitalSmarts revealed that employees who keep silent about a problem, process, or strategy that just isn't working out—often because they're worried about being labeled as complainers or because they fear retaliation—costs companies in terms of productivity. Most workers in the survey blamed their workplace culture for making them too scared to speak up. Almost half (46 percent) expected retaliation for reporting something; 45 percent didn't think any of their colleagues would support them, leaving them socially stranded; and 37 percent were afraid that speaking up would brand them as a complainer, hurting their careers.[54]

To encourage employees to speak up, the study recommends that leaders employ strategies like establishing safe channels, such as a company hotline, to encourage employees to report issues without fear of retribution."[55]

Poorly Organized Meetings Waste Time and Money

New and veteran employees alike often feel frustrated about having to participate in meetings that seem pointless.

An online scheduling service called Doodle studied 19 million meetings and discovered that the cost of poorly organized meetings in 2019 was expected to reach $399 billion in the United States. Bad meetings cause a diversion of attention from employees' work, a loss of focus on projects, and inefficient processes that weaken client/supplier relationships. The authors of the report offered suggestions for improving meetings, such as following an agenda for every meeting and using visual stimuli such as videos.[56]

As you gain longevity at your company, you can make a valuable contribution toward helping your peers conduct meetings that are more efficient, organized, and useful. However, the advice in this chapter is more about attending meetings than it is about organizing or running meetings.

If you are new to your company or to the workforce, you probably won't be asked to chair a meeting until you have gained some experience. However, if your job does require you to conduct meetings, plenty of resources are available online that can help you gain insights on organizing and chairing a meeting.

For example, a 2019 article from The Balance Careers website explains how to plan a meeting, enable group involvement, handle logistics, record meeting minutes, solve problems during a meeting, build consensus, and more.[57]

The advice that follows is from different perspectives, depending on your role as a participant in a business meeting. I recommend anyone who attends a meeting at their place of work should always strive to overprepare. Also note that the following tips for attending and participating in meetings apply to relatively small group meetings in which anyone in the room might participate in the discussions. They are not meant to apply to large group meetings like conventions or all-hands-on-deck town hall meetings. Although these tips can apply to large group meetings, the focus of this chapter is on smaller meetings in which active participation is likely to be expected or encouraged.

Tips for Anyone Attending a Meeting

"If any of you lacks wisdom, you should ask God, who gives generously to all without finding fault, and it will be given to you."
—James 1:5

If you are invited to a meeting, you are likely to receive some form of communication inviting you to attend. The invitation will probably include an agenda that will provide you with some basic information like the following:

- The date, time, and location of the meeting
- The purpose or objectives of the meeting
- The topics to be covered and who will cover each of them
- A list of other invitees
- Attachments containing materials to be read in advance of the meeting

Your tendency might be to worry later about the specifics related to the meeting. However, I encourage you to prepare early so you have adequate time to be ready to participate. This will reduce any anxiety you might be feeling about the meeting.

Consider doing the following for each of the above pieces of information that are likely to be included in the invitation.

1. The Date, Time, and Location of the Meeting

In addition to making sure your calendar is clear for the meeting date and time, also consider what is on your calendar already on that date, and immediately before the meeting time, to be certain that you won't risk being late for the meeting. You might need a one- or two-hour buffer before the meeting to gather your thoughts and read or reread any previously distributed materials.

It is even beneficial to look at the meeting room so you can assess how the physical space might impact the human interactions during the meeting. For example, will audiovisual aids be used? What is the seating configuration? Will everyone easily be able to see everyone else? Are there chairs around the perimeter of the room, where the inactive observers are likely to be seated? Where is the closest restroom? Becoming familiar with all these details will make you much more relaxed and comfortable when you attend the meeting.

2. The Purpose or Objectives of the Meeting

It is critically important to know in advance of the meeting what the purpose is and what the intended outcomes will be. If that is not clear in the invitation, then don't hesitate to call the organizer of the meeting to find out. If necessary, ask to set up a meeting or make a phone call to the organizer to gain clarity.

That will allow you to better understand why you have been invited. Even if you are not expected to be an active participant or a presenter at the meeting, you can begin to think about how you can contribute and what further reading or research you need to do to get up to speed and maybe even to make a meaningful contribution to the discussions during the meeting.

3. The Topics to Be Covered and Who Will Cover Each of Them

Next, look at the topics to be discussed at the meeting and who the presenters will be. If no material is provided for advance reading, or if you feel you aren't knowledgeable on the topic, consider asking for reading material. If it still is not clear to you, set up a meeting with one or more of the presenters to ask a few questions before the meeting. You don't want to take up a lot of time in the meeting asking questions to which most others in the room already know the answers.

This kind of inquiry on your part serves multiple purposes. It demonstrates your commitment, it can expand your network to other departments and individuals, and it increases your knowledge of the business. I did this often throughout my career.

4. A List of Other Invitees

The meeting invitation you receive might include the topics to be covered and the names of the presenters. Look to see if some of the other invitees might be attending but not presenting.

If you have never met some of them, use this opportunity to connect with them, to determine their roles in the company, and to get their perspectives on the meeting. If you are unclear about why you were invited to the meeting, speaking to others can provide further insights.

5. Attachments Containing Materials to Be Read in Advance of the Meeting

The organizer of the meeting will expect all participants to have read all materials provided in advance of the meeting. It is imperative that you do so. If there is anything you don't understand, follow up with the appropriate individual before the meeting to get answers to your questions. Even if you say nothing at the meeting, this understanding will enable you to personally gain much more from the experience.

Tips for an Inactive Participant

"Cast all your anxiety on him because he cares for you."
—1 Peter 5:7

If you have been invited to a meeting and you are not a presenter, and not expected to be an active participant, it is probably because someone either thinks you can learn from the experience or you can contribute ideas either at the meeting or afterward. Try to understand which it is before the meeting by speaking to your direct supervisor. Either way, feel pleased that you have been invited, even if it is a little difficult to determine why you are there.

1. Identify Questions That Might Be Directed to You during the Meeting

Once you understand the purpose and objectives of the meeting and who all the presenters and attendees will be, think of all the possible questions that someone might ask you. Be ready with answers. This exercise might surface additional questions you may have or ideas of ways in which you can contribute during the meeting.

2. Identify Any Pertinent Comments You Might Make at the Meeting

If you have determined that you have been invited as an inactive participant, then be extremely sure of yourself if you plan to make a comment or suggestion. It is risky to do so if you haven't tested the idea before the meeting with one of the presenters. I strongly encourage you to do so. If you feel it is appropriate to interject a comment during the meeting, then ask the leader of the meeting for permission to speak.

In your first meeting or two with a given group, you might have what you believe is a great question or comment but then decide not to speak up. Many times during my career, I found that someone else asked the great question I didn't ask or made the great comment I didn't make. Don't second-guess yourself. If someone else makes a brilliant comment that you could have made, consider it reassuring that you understood the discussion. That will give you confidence to speak up at future meetings.

3. Take Notes

Even if you are not asked to take notes, do so anyway, for yourself. Highlight in your notes details you don't totally understand and will need to follow up on. Your notes will prove to be of value if there are subsequent meetings on the same topics, especially if no one provides detailed minutes after the meeting. Even when minutes are provided, I have often found them to be woefully inadequate. I would caution you, however, not to overdo this. Don't bury yourself into your note taking. You want to appear fully engaged and interested in what is being said so you need to make frequent eye contact with presenters and others, even if you never utter a word during the meeting.

Tips for an Active Participant

"Finally, all of you, be like-minded, be sympathetic, love one another, be compassionate and humble."
—1 Peter 3:8

If you are invited because you are expected to actively participate in the discussions, do the following in addition to the tips just mentioned for inactive participants.

1. Speak to the Organizer of the Meeting to Understand Your Role

Speak to the organizer of the meeting to be clear about what is expected of you. Ask if you will be a presenter and if so, how much time will be allotted to your topic. Determine if you should distribute written documents before the meeting and if a slide presentation or handouts would be appropriate at the meeting.

2. Prepare Your Presentation if You Are Asked to Present

If you are expected to make a presentation, then follow the advice in chapter 13 on making every presentation a command performance.

3. Write Out Questions and Comments for All Topics

After you have reviewed all the advance reading material for each of the agenda items, write down all the questions you have or the comments you might make for each topic. I always wrote these on a single sheet of paper for easy reference during the meeting.

Cautionary Advice

Early in your career, attendance at meetings is a learning experience, as opposed to an opportunity to display your knowledge. Don't risk appearing arrogant by leaping into the conversation inappropriately—perceived arrogance is a major career blocker.

———

Because many people consider meetings to be a waste of time, they often show up unprepared and/or with a negative mind-set. By viewing every meeting as an opportunity to gain knowledge, and by overpreparing, you will distinguish yourself as a valuable employee with strong potential.

CHAPTER 13

MAKE EVERY PRESENTATION
A COMMAND PERFORMANCE

*"In the same way, let your light shine before others, so that they may
see your good works and give glory to your Father who is in heaven."*
—Matthew 5:16 (ESV)

When you are fortunate enough to be asked to make a presentation of any kind, always consider it a command performance. Seize the opportunity to show off your talents (but not in an arrogant way).

Throughout my career, I encountered many people who treated their presentations as a necessary but unwelcome job responsibility. It was as if they considered their presentations to be annoyances that interfered with their "real" work. And like a trip to the dentist, they were glad when it was completed, and the pain subsided.

I held the opposite view. I have always believed that presentations provide you with an opportunity to showcase your knowledge and expertise; to lead, guide, and inform others; and to contribute to an organization's success.

For that reason, I always put a lot of thought and effort into my presentations—whether they were short presentations to a small group of employees or more in-depth presentations to a much larger group. Larger groups were often employees of a large division or department, a large "town hall" type meeting, or a presentation addressed to thousands of the company's agents. As my career advanced, I also had numerous opportunities to speak at industry meetings and eventually was honored to deliver a few college commencement addresses.

I gave the same level of attention to my preparation for each presentation, no matter what the audience or venue. In this chapter, I provide you with some useful tips on your own preparation.

The one constant throughout my career, before every such presentation, was to call on God to guide me through His Holy Spirit in what to say and how to deliver the message. Even as a seasoned presenter, I always was nervous before presentations, but I relied on the Holy Spirit to calm my nerves and to give me the right things to say.

> *"But the Advocate, the Holy Spirit, whom the Father will send in my name, will teach you all things and will remind you of everything I have said to you."*
> —John 14:26

Following every presentation, I always thanked God for His assistance, even at times when I felt I had said something that was not clear and was possibly misinterpreted. In those situations, I learned from my mistakes and avoided repeating them. I viewed those experiences not as the Holy Spirit failing me in the presentation, but rather as God enhancing my development and evolution as a better communicator.

Speaking Skills Are High on Employers' Wish Lists

Did you ever notice, when watching interviews or presentations delivered by high-ranking corporate executives or government officials, that in most cases, they are very articulate, and their remarks are well-structured? There most certainly is a positive correlation between success and speaking ability.

In a 2018 survey conducted by the Association of American Colleges and Universities, executives and hiring managers said good verbal communication is the skill they want most from job candidates. This skill outranked others that get far more public attention, such as critical thinking, solving complex problems, working in teams, and writing well. More than 80 percent of the executives and hiring managers surveyed said good verbal skills were important, and fewer than half said recent college graduates excel in this area.[58]

A primary reason why schools don't focus on this important skill is that schools are not generally required to test for it. This means that, most likely, you will need to develop your own speaking and presentation skills.

This is an area in which new employees (especially those re-entering the workforce after an absence) can most easily position themselves for career success. In the sections that follow, I will point out ways in which you can benefit by greatly enhancing these critical skills. If you are re-entering the workforce after an extended absence, you probably were schooled in an earlier era, when there was more emphasis in schools on communication and public speaking skills. If so, that may give you a head start and an early advantage.

What Makes a Great Presentation?

A lot goes into a great presentation, and there are several key steps that need to be executed with utmost professionalism and attention to detail. This advice is relevant whether your presentation is scheduled to be three minutes long or three hours long. I have actually found that it is often more challenging to deliver a highly effective short message than it is to deliver a much longer presentation.

That has been true for centuries. In 1657, the French mathematician and philosopher Blaise Pascal wrote this famous statement in a letter that later appeared in a collection called *Lettres Provinciales*: "I have made this longer than usual because I have not had time to make it shorter."[59]

I have learned how to be an effective presenter the hard way—by making many mistakes in my early career presentations. I have written this book to help you to avoid my mistakes and learn from my successes. The same could be said of every topic covered in chapters 6 through 15 of this book. You might not implement everything I have suggested, but by reading the book and being aware of what works and what doesn't, you should benefit significantly.

When you couple the knowledge you will gain with your faith, your prayers, and your reliance on the guidance of the Holy Spirit, I am confident you will have a happy and successful work experience throughout your career.

Here are a few preliminary recommendations as you begin to plan for your presentation:

1. **Know your audience.** It is important for you to know the interest level of the audience you will be addressing and their level of knowledge and competency in the subject matter. You can't always gear your remarks to everyone in the audience, but you want to make sure the majority of those in attendance will

understand what you are saying and will be glad they attended the session.

As an actuary, I often was overly technical; used PowerPoint slides that were much too dense with numbers, charts, and graphics; and assumed that my audience had technical actuarial knowledge that, often, they did not have.

2. **Be familiar with the venue and how much time is allotted for your remarks.** To the extent possible, in advance of any presentation, make sure you are familiar with the room, the acoustics in the room, whether or not you will need a microphone, and whether or not the set-up in the room will accommodate slides or other audiovisual aids. Determine this information before you begin to construct your remarks.

It is important to know the amount of time you will be allotted. I always resisted presentations that were expected to be longer than twenty or twenty-five minutes because I was aware of studies indicating that no matter how good your presentation is, it will be difficult to hold an audience's attention for longer than that amount of time. If a much longer time is required, as it would be for a seminar or a class you are teaching, include several scheduled breaks.

Guidelines vary on how often you should give your audience a break. The International Institute for Facilitation and Change (IIFAC) offers these recommendations:[60]

- For multi-hour sessions, schedule a break at least every ninety minutes.
- Breaks should last fifteen to thirty minutes, depending on the size of the group and the meeting context.
- "Bio breaks" of five to ten minutes allow participants time to go to the bathroom, drink water, and stretch their legs. But the facilitator needs to make it clear

that this is not a long break and that the meeting will resume promptly.

3. **Key points.** Identify in advance the four or five key points you want your audience to remember. In an oral presentation, a list of dozens of ideas won't be memorable and will only frustrate members of the audience. I have given numerous presentations to college students about how to enter the workforce. In those presentations, I typically cull down the number of fast-start tips or strategies from the fifteen in this book to no more than five.

4. **Research.** It is best to speak on topics for which you are considered an expert. If you have any doubts about your command of a particular topic, then you will need to do some research to better prepare yourself. If there will be a question-and-answer (Q&A) session at the end of your remarks, then try to think through, in advance, the questions that are most likely to be asked, and be prepared with answers. Have a friend or colleague watch you rehearse the speech, provide useful advice, and ask questions that audience members might ask. If you get a question for which you don't know the answer, don't be afraid to say you don't know the answer but will get back to that person with an answer. Never try to wing it with an off-the-cuff answer that you aren't very confident about.

5. **Maximizing memorable impact on your audience.** Your presentation should focus on the topic you've been asked to discuss. I once was given a great tip on how to structure a presentation to have maximum impact. The tip was to deliver the key message three times. At the beginning, tell your audience what you plan to discuss; then in the body of your presentation, discuss it; and at the end, close by recapping what you told them. In this way, the audience knows what's coming, they hear it, and then they are reminded of your key points.

That advice is echoed in the old adage that says, "Tell 'em what you're going to tell 'em, tell 'em, and then tell 'em what you told 'em."[61] I believe this is true—being clear about the key message you will discuss helps your audience understand and retain the main points. Repetition is the key to retention.

As you are preparing your presentation, keep your overall objective in mind. Is it purely informational? Is your objective to persuade them to subscribe to your point of view? Is it to trigger specific actions by those in your audience? It may be a combination of two or even all three of these outcomes.

6. **Visual appeal.** If visual aids are called for, whether you use PowerPoint, Prezi, or another presentation program, make sure your presentation has a lot of visual appeal. Where appropriate, include interactive elements, such as links to YouTube or other videos, to hold the interest of your audience. On each slide, include an interesting heading/title and a few bullet points. Avoid filling the slides with text or excessive amounts of numbers. Text-heavy slides are difficult to read, especially for the people in the back of the room. Include photos, a pleasing color palette, quotes, and other appealing visuals.

   A study of more than two thousand professionals in the United States found that the key to creating engaging content is to combine a compelling narrative with stimulating visuals and dialogue. The survey dispels the common belief that people's attention spans are shrinking in this era of Twitter and texting. The survey found that people's ability to maintain focus has actually *improved* over time, despite an ever-growing mountain of available content.[62]

7. **Delivery.** Practice your presentation until you can deliver it comfortably without reading from your notes. Be enthusiastic.

Showcase your knowledge. And again, keep your original objective in mind as you are speaking.

8. **Clarification.** Allow a few minutes for a Q&A session. Giving your audience a chance to ask questions, and then answering them concisely but thoroughly, will provide clarification about any details your audience didn't fully understand.

Storytelling Is a Key to Effective Presentations

Think about the most compelling presentation you've ever heard. Whether it was a life lesson your grandfather taught you as a kid, a pep talk from a coach in high school or college, or a TED Talk you heard on YouTube, chances are, the key ingredient was storytelling. When you tell a story to make a point, it will be much more interesting than if you simply present facts and data. Plus, your audience is much more likely to remember your key point if you tell a story. Stories enhance message retention.

Kindra Hall makes this point in her book *Stories That Stick: How Storytelling Can Captivate Customers, Influence Audiences, and Transform Your Business*. Hall explains why stories are so effective for presenting ideas, findings, or recommendations: "Decision makers are inundated with data, and they're much more likely to remember a story than a graph on a slide."[63]

The author of a 2019 *Forbes* article who relayed some of Hall's strategies wrote, "Being able to influence an audience of one or one hundred is universally vital in today's competitive professional marketplace, and storytelling can be such an effective technique to build those critical influence skills."[64]

How to Construct Your Presentation

In this section, I outline for you the process I almost always followed to construct a presentation and then prepare to deliver the speech. You might decide there are some steps you don't need to take once you become proficient at giving presentations, or when you find yourself repeating a presentation many times to similar audiences. This might be the case for politicians running for office or for professors teaching a course multiple times. But for many of us, each presentation and each audience often has unique characteristics.

Here are the steps I typically followed:

1. Know your audience.
2. Know your subject matter; if you don't, then do the necessary research.
3. Identify the four or five key points you want the audience to remember.
4. Construct an outline of the flow of your presentation. Often, mine looked something like this:
   A. Thank the audience for their attendance and for inviting you to speak.
   B. Start with humor. Getting a laugh from the audience up-front is a great way to calm your own nerves.
   C. Tell the audience what you plan to cover and what you think they will benefit most from hearing. It's OK to even tell them briefly what your conclusions will be.
   D. In the main body of your presentation, elaborate on the four or five key points and why they are important.
   E. If appropriate, give the audience a call to action.
   F. Make closing remarks, reiterating the key points, conclusions, and their importance to the audience and the company.
5. Once you have an outline, write out your speech. For me, this was an extremely important step. However, let me be clear—I

want to emphatically advise you never to simply read a speech, unless for some reason you are forced to use a teleprompter.

6. To rehearse, read the written speech out loud, just as if you were delivering it live. When you do this, you will find yourself making many changes to key words and points of emphasis.

7. Repeat step 7 again after making modifications, and time yourself. You will probably make even more modifications in this step.

8. Transform the written speech into bullet points. Initially, these might be quite long. Boldface or underline the key words in each bullet point.

9. Now try delivering the speech from the bullet points without reading. Do this two or three times.

10. Shorten the bullet points again, and practice the talk out loud two or three more times. Each time you rehearse a delivery, if you are like me, you will further shorten the written bullet points.

By following the above process, I often gave thirty-minute (or longer) presentations using only an outline of key topics and key words on a single 4-inch by 6-inch index card. In fact, many times, the card was only a failsafe backup, and I didn't really need to glance at it.

Rehearsing your talk using this process will help you create an excellent flow to your talk, enhance your spontaneity, and reinforce your command of the subject matter.

A Final Word: Texting and Social Media

Now that texting and social media are preferred communication venues, especially for younger people, everyday language has become truncated and filled with acronyms. It could be easy for people who didn't grow up in a texting and social-media environment to fear that this abbreviated form of language might ruin kids' communication skills forever.

That isn't necessarily true, though. In a study of ten- to thirteen-year-olds, researchers found that most kids who used "textisms" still used proper grammar where it counts—in schoolwork. They found that kids knew it was OK to abbreviate words and use slang in text messages to friends but that they needed to use proper spelling and grammar in the real world.[65]

Today, for the first time in history, we have five generations working side by side in organizations worldwide. The key to communicating effectively across generational lines—and with individuals—is to be aware of each person's preferred communication style.[66]

Some older people might consider text-speak to be inappropriate for business presentations, and some younger people might not resonate well with presentations they consider too formal and stodgy. So it's important to achieve a balance. If you are re-entering the workplace and had traditional training in public speaking, that could give you a head start and an advantage in terms of getting over stage fright and speaking persuasively with confidence. However, it's possible that your manager and some of your co-workers might be younger than you, in which case it will be helpful to understand—or at least not reject—their preferred style of communication.

In late 2019, one report noted that 38 percent of Americans worked for a boss who was younger than them.[67]

Excellent presentation skills are essential in the workplace, whether you are returning to the workplace after an absence or are working in your first job out of college. And proper English, complete with punctuation and capitalization, will never go out of style!

CHAPTER 14

DEMONSTRATE INTEGRITY AND EARN TRUST

"The integrity of the upright guides them, but the crookedness of the treacherous destroys them."
—Proverbs 11:3 (ESV)

Integrity and trustworthiness are qualities that are essential to future success in any career. In this chapter, I elaborate on some ways you can earn trust and demonstrate integrity. Few people focus on how to convey those qualities. Rather, they often simply rely on the ability of superiors, peers, and subordinates to discern those characteristics in them.

I have found that the perception that a person is arrogant can be a significant barrier to his or her success in the workplace. Examples of how arrogance can be conveyed might surprise some people. People can convey arrogance inadvertently by the way they dress, their body language, the words they use, how they react under stress or when being confronted, and even how they carry themselves.

I have successfully coached many people on how to demonstrate integrity and earn trust. In addition, I have coached and mentored several young people on how to avoid the death knell of arrogance. Dealing with these issues (which often are largely perceptual) is particularly gratifying and meaningful for those who profess their Christianity yet don't realize they are inadvertently projecting the wrong persona.

Displaying Integrity in the Workplace

"For we are taking pains to do what is right, not only in the eyes of the Lord but also in the eyes of man."
—2 Corinthians 8:21

As you come to understand the culture of your own company or a company at which you hope to secure employment, you may or may not find that the company intentionally identifies integrity as a corporate value and makes it a part of its everyday practices.

A climate of honesty and trust that is fostered and communicated from the top can be quite effective. It sends a message to employees and customers that exhibiting these characteristics is a priority.

But even if you aren't so fortunate to work for a company that explicitly identifies integrity as an important core value, it is extremely important for you to demonstrate integrity as an individual.

The really great leaders of our time, whether in business or in any other profession, almost all seem to exhibit one consistent character trait: integrity. They serve as role models of integrity by doing what's right, no matter what the circumstances may be. They do what they say they will do. Often, they are devoid of personal agendas as they focus on the greater good of their companies and the customers or people they serve.

How to Display Integrity

Even if you consider integrity to be one of your core values, your integrity won't be apparent to those around you unless you take actions that display your integrity. Here are some ways to do that.

1. Be Honest

You've heard it said that "honesty is the best policy." That is as true in your work life as it is in your personal life. Of course this means avoiding lies, but it also means avoiding exaggeration or even putting an inappropriately positive spin on a negative result. We all want to put our best foot forward, especially in sales and marketing materials, but you cross the line when you stretch the truth. Strive to always convey information or results with equal precision, whether that information is positive or negative.

I used an expression with my employees that encouraged and welcomed full disclosure of bad news as well as good. I let them know I valued their willingness to "tell me what I needed to know, not what I wanted to hear." I couldn't deal with a problem I didn't know existed. So I genuinely wanted to know all bad news or emerging bad news so I could deal with it before it became a more serious problem.

Gain this understanding with your superiors, peers, and subordinates. In my view, withholding or sugar-coating negative information is a form of dishonesty that can have potentially bad consequences.

2. Keep Your Word and Your Commitments

You will develop a reputation of integrity if you are meticulous about delivering on your promises and fulfilling your commitments.

If you say you are going to do something, do it. Make every effort to complete it within the committed time frame.

I strongly caution you not to make the mistake of overcommitting to promises you might not be able to fulfill. If this happens, you will quickly develop the opposite reputation to the one you are trying to establish

3. Be Accountable and Take Responsibility

Inevitably, you will make mistakes at work. The best way to display integrity is to admit to a mistake. Apologize if it has hurt someone else or damaged a relationship.

Your reputation will flourish if you make a practice of "giving credit and taking blame." Even if a bad result is because of a team failure, consider taking the blame yourself. And whatever you do, don't claim that you are solely responsible for major team accomplishments. At all levels in organizations, I have often encountered people who do the opposite: They "give blame and take credit."

Building Trust in the Workplace

"Let a man regard us in this manner, as servants of Christ and stewards of the mysteries of God. In this case, moreover, it is required of stewards that one be found trustworthy."
—1 Corinthians 4:1–2 (NASB)

According to a 2019 survey from Pew Research, 64 percent of Americans think their trust in each other has been shrinking. Almost half of Americans (49 percent) link the decline in interpersonal trust to a belief that people are not as reliable as they used to be. Many ascribe shrinking trust to a political culture they believe is broken and spawns suspicion, even cynicism, about the ability of others to distinguish fact from fiction.[68]

But Americans are optimistic that trust among one another can be restored. The majority—86 percent—believe the level of confidence Americans have in the federal government and each other can be improved. Solutions they offer include spending more time with people and practicing empathy.[69]

Whether in politics, business relationships, or our personal lives, trust is an essential component of healthy relationships. The more we can do to build trust among those around us, the more we can thrive.

In the workplace, teams accomplish so much that it is essential to your reputation, your success, and the company's success that participants in a team effort trust one another.

It requires a conscious effort to maximize the probability of earning the trust of others. The success of a team-oriented project requires that the participants rely on each other. That reliance is best facilitated through mutual trust.

How to Earn Others' Trust

Follow these tips to build trust with your peers, subordinates, and superiors.

1. Praise the Work Others Do

Be quick to praise others in the workplace and give them credit for their work. In so doing, you will build trust and be perceived as a gracious person. While it may seem difficult to do this for someone whom you may perceive as a competitor of yours, it will go a long way toward establishing a strong working relationship.

2. Avoid Complaining or Gossiping

There is no quicker way to be distrusted than to be a complainer or a gossiper. Gossip is potentially lethal to a good relationship. Even if you are complaining or gossiping about others and the subject of your gossip or complaint never finds out about it (which is unlikely), the people you are complaining to will almost certainly wonder if you are also complaining or gossiping about them to others.

If you seem to be developing misunderstandings or issues with coworkers, try to resolve them in private conversations with them rather than talking to others about the issues. I have found that in a well-thought-out and calm discussion, resolution almost always occurs because the other person realizes you really care about the relationship.

3. Show Trust in Others

This seems pretty obvious, but it really is true that if you demonstrate trust in others, they are likely to reciprocate. Until they prove otherwise, trust your coworkers to execute tasks they say they will do, to meet committed deadlines, and to be honest.

If you are in a position that requires you to manage other employees, you will inadvertently communicate distrust by constantly watching over them or micromanaging. You obviously need to monitor progress, but not by pestering them daily. I typically had regularly scheduled meetings with each of my direct reports only twice each month to track progress.

4. Avoid Displaying Negative Body Language

Use body language as a trust builder and sustainer, as opposed to a trust destroyer. It can be difficult to control your body language, but making a concerted effort to do so will go a long way to establishing trusting relationships.

Our faces and our posture often convey negative messages to someone who is speaking to us. Frowns, negative head nods, and even what we do with our eyebrows can communicate disagreement, skepticism, and anger. Sitting with your arms crossed on your chest or slouching in your chair can communicate an unwillingness to listen, disinterest, or disagreement.

Reacting to what someone else says by laughing at it or scoffing is likely to cause them to think twice about sharing ideas in the future. It might even shut down effective communications.

Conversely, positive body language such as smiling, making eye contact, nodding your head affirmatively, and leaning into the conversation will make your coworkers comfortable. It will make them feel connected with you and will make them willing to engage more fully in providing their opinions and offering new ideas.

5. Treat Your Coworkers with Respect and Dignity

Remind yourself often that as a Christian, you recognize the worth of every human being. Someone's title or job grade doesn't change that fundamental belief. Reflect that in how you treat everyone, whether they are the CEO or someone from the custodial staff. Remember that in the eyes of the Lord, everyone else is just as important as you are.

If you fail to treat anyone in your organization with respect and dignity, it will be noticed, and you will risk conveying arrogance. That can be a devastating roadblock to your future advancement. There's more on the topic of arrogance below.

6. Be Humble and Occasionally Self-Deprecating

Great leaders in any field, including business, often exhibit great humility, understate their accomplishments, and even joke about their shortcomings. Being self-deprecating shows people that you do not consider yourself to be superior to them.

The litmus test of leadership is if others will follow. Think about your own life experiences. How inclined are you to follow someone who displays a powerful ego, demands perfection from his or her workers, and brags about personal accomplishments while giving little credit to employees? We all have known people like this. In my experience, they are more likely to fail than to succeed by almost any measure.

The following are just a few characteristics, qualities, and behaviors that will enable you to convey humility in the workplace:

- Admit when you are wrong.
- Take responsibility for your failures.
- Give credit to others for successes.
- Ask for others' opinions on important matters.
- Be a good listener.
- Exhibit compassion and exercise kindness.

Avoiding Arrogance in the Workplace

"For an overseer, as God's steward, must be above reproach. He must not be arrogant or quick-tempered or a drunkard or violent or greedy for gain."
—Titus 1:7 (ESV)

In my view, arrogance is one of the greatest career blockers and one of the most difficult perceptions to overcome. Part of the reason is that often, arrogance is conveyed by body language and by inadvertent behaviors that others perceive as arrogant. For that reason, it is particularly difficult to coach someone on how to avoid appearing arrogant, especially if they are already perceived as such.

The Merriam-Webster dictionary defines *arrogant* as *"having or showing the insulting attitude of people who believe that they are better, smarter, or more important than others."*

As we talk about how to avoid or overcome arrogance, remember that in the above dictionary definition, the key phrase in the definition of arrogance is an "insulting attitude."

Don't confuse confidence with arrogance. Merriam-Webster defines *confidence* as "faith or belief that one will act in a right, proper, or effective way." There is nothing insulting about a healthy level of confidence. In fact, confidence can inspire coworkers and can enable you and the others in your organization to develop a collaborative work environment that enables you to get things done. But arrogance turns people off and makes them far less collaborative.

How Do You Know if You Are Perceived as Arrogant?

I have worked with a number of people who had no idea that they were perceived as arrogant. As mentioned, once that perception exists, it is difficult to reverse it. So here are some ways to self-reflect on the possibility that you might be exhibiting some of the common characteristics of arrogant people.

The trick to mitigating this perception is to become aware of arrogance, try to avoid or stop it, and transform it, whenever possible, into a more positive, productive behavioral trait. Consider your answers to these questions:

- Do you find yourself impatient and unwilling to listen to others?
- Do you believe that most people are not up to your level of intelligence?
- Do you tend to dominate conversations and even interrupt others when you have what you believe is a better point to make?
- Do you view most others as competitors instead of equals?
- Do you take credit for successes and blame others for failures?
- Do you patronize others by using language that can be perceived as condescending?
- Do you display an attitude of superiority, as if other people's ideas and opinions don't matter?
- Do you use the words "I" and "me" much more than "we" and "us"?

- Do you generally think that your way is the right way?
- Do you seem to have a lot of enemies?

If you answered "yes" to any of these questions, it is an indication that some of your actions, and your attitude, might come across to others as arrogance. Monitor your own attitude and behaviors carefully, and avoid those tendencies.

Overcoming Arrogance

In addition to avoiding the behaviors and traits noted above, consciously take the following steps to avoid arrogance and even potentially reverse the perception over time.

1. Recognize That You Are Human

You will make mistakes, and you are a work in progress. Occasionally poke fun at yourself.

2. Listen to and Value Other People's Points of View

If you value and thoughtfully consider other opinions, you will build stronger relationships with, and earn the respect of, your coworkers.

3. Avoid Having an Attitude of Entitlement

Recognize that you should not demand, nor do you deserve, special treatment. No one does.

4. Be Considerate of Others

Avoid dominating every conversation and inappropriately interrupting others. Never take advantage of your rank in a way that inconveniences others. Doing so will stifle your potential for leadership roles because no one will want to follow you.

5. Avoid Belittling Others

I have witnessed many examples of public humiliation. This is never acceptable. If you ever do it, it will render you an ineffective leader with no respect from others and no following. Reprimanding a subordinate or colleague in an open forum embarrasses and demotivates the person in question, and it makes others fear displeasing you. People will begin to tell you what you want to hear instead of what you need to know. A team of sycophants can be dangerous and counterproductive. As a manager, remember to praise in public or in private, but always correct or reprimand someone in private.

6. Be Gracious

Go out of your way to praise the good work of others, no matter what their level in the organization. Doing so communicates that you have noticed them and that you value what they do. You'll be surprised at how quickly the word will get out that you are a gracious person. That reputation will attract others to you. It might even result in having others open up to you with new ideas because they know you'll listen.

An employee who demonstrates integrity, is trustworthy, and is confident but not arrogant is far more likely to succeed and advance in an organization than an employee who does not possess these qualities.

———

As mentioned in an earlier chapter, employers can teach technical skills, but they cannot teach valuable "soft" skills like integrity and trust. Demonstrating that you possess, and value, these characteristics will lay a solid foundation for your effectiveness and value to your organization.

CHAPTER 15

BALANCE FAITH, FAMILY, AND CAREER

"But as for me and my household, we will serve the LORD."
—Joshua 24:15

As I indicated in the opening of chapter 10, I consider this chapter second in importance only behind Part 1 (chapters 1–5, biblical principles in the workplace). Given the importance of this chapter, please indulge me as I share some of my own priorities and experiences related to this topic. This is not an attempt to aggrandize myself but rather to use my spiritual gifts to positively impact your life—something I described earlier in this book as my greatest passion.

Recently, Jack Krasula of WJR radio in Detroit interviewed me. Jack has interviewed hundreds of Christians, many of whom have also been successful in business. We have become good friends. In one of our many luncheon meetings, he asked me to send him a note that succinctly describes my philosophy of life.

What I sent to him (below) is what I believe to be a guide to living a happy and fulfilled life:

Philosophy of Life

I believe to realize happiness and fulfillment in life, you must:

1. Identify your spiritual gifts and use them to serve the Lord.
2. Study the teachings of Jesus Christ and live your life as He would have you live it.
3. Love God with all your heart, mind, and soul.
4. Love your neighbor as yourself.
5. Love yourself.

With that philosophy as a backdrop, now I offer some guidance about setting priorities and balancing your life.

In this day and age, whether you are in the early stages of your career or you have advanced into greater responsibilities, the demands on your time can be quite extreme.

With today's technology, we are hyperconnected to other people and to seemingly infinite amounts of data and information, available to us in a millisecond. But we all seem to be more overworked, less productive, and lonelier than ever.

RescueTime, an automated time-tracking software program, analyzed 185 million working hours of anonymized and aggregated data from its users to find out how they spent their time in 2018. Here are some highlights from that research:[70]

- 21 percent of working hours are spent on entertainment, news, and social media.

- 40 percent of people use their computers after 10:00 p.m.
- 26 percent of work is done outside normal working hours.
- Workers average at least 1 hour of work outside working hours 89 days/year (and on 50 percent of all weekend days).
- We check email and Instant Messaging, on average, every 6 minutes.
- 40.1 percent of our day is spent multitasking with communication tools.

It all boils down to priorities. We are inundated with expectations, responsibilities, and self-exerted pressure to succeed to the point where we try to do everything well, all at once. It's just not possible. Quality is more important than quantity. We need to focus on what's truly important in our lives—often a balance of faith, family, and career—and a prioritization of those elements in our daily schedules.

Another example of spiritual sharing and disclosure of my priorities was something I mentioned in presentations I made as the president of the New York Life Insurance Company to all sizes of audiences of agents, employees, and even members of the company's Board of Directors. I indicated in those presentations, as well as in numerous radio and TV interviews following the publication of my first two books, that the following have consistently been my top five priorities:

1. My relationship with God (as a Christian, that is more specifically my personal relationship with Christ).
2. My relationship with my wife, Sue
3. My relationship with my children and my extended family
4. My job
5. My volunteer and leisure activities

Imagine the president of a Fortune 100 company listing the job as fourth on his or her personal priority list. But that's exactly what I did.

Your list will probably differ somewhat from mine, but defining your priorities helps you articulate them in writing and reminds you of them regularly. In that way, they will be top of mind. And if you start to reorder them, whether intentionally or not, you'll realize that you need to return them to their proper sequence.

For many of us, not just top executives, our jobs sometimes demand a higher ranking. That is to be expected, but it's important to give your job no more than a temporary repositioning.

The pressures in the current environment are enormous and can easily cause us to ignore important priorities. Let me go on to discuss those pressures and some coping techniques I have successfully deployed.

The Dangerous Consequences of Overextending Yourself

Most companies have become more aggressive in pursuing higher profitability. One way to achieve that, in addition to greater revenue growth, is through cost reduction. Yet, despite significant improvements in technology in recent years, employees at all levels continue to be expected to produce more with fewer and fewer resources—including human resources. The output expected from an individual today is multiples of what was expected from an individual just a few years ago.

The unintended negative consequence and collateral damage from this environment is the negative impact on our personal and family lives.

According to numerous studies by Marianna Virtanen of the Finnish Institute of Occupational Health, overwork and the resulting stress can lead to all sorts of health problems, including the following:[71]

- Impaired sleep
- Depression

- Heavy drinking
- Diabetes
- Impaired memory
- Heart disease

The more hours we work, the less healthy we become. This is a costly outcome for our own health and our relationships as individuals. It's also detrimental to a company's bottom line because the consequences of overwork lead to increased absenteeism and turnover, decreased productivity, and rising employee dissatisfaction.

Productivity decreases when we scatter our attention. So how can we stay focused?

Coping Techniques to Help You Focus on What's Important

While I was serving as the president of New York Life, a large Fortune 100 company headquartered in Manhattan, I was also active in my church and busy as a husband and a father of five children. Over the years, I developed a number of coping techniques that allowed me to effectively balance faith, family, and career. I have heard many effective coping techniques from people who have attended numerous small-group speaking engagements I conducted after writing my first two books. In those sessions, I would often start by talking about my coping techniques and then ask participants (mostly "bedroom community" Type A executives and employees) if they had any to share.

Years ago, I had a true epiphany about the importance of making time for family. It has been the most important technique to my family and me. The best way for me to share the impact of this coping technique is to share with you an abbreviated version of a story titled "The Accidental Legacy" from chapter 6 of my first book, *God Revealed*.

The Accidental Legacy[72]

In the mid-1980s, after several years of working long hours and regretfully neglecting my family, I became the senior vice president and CFO of Maccabees Mutual Life Insurance Company in Southfield, Michigan. My career aspirations were coming to fruition, but other dimensions of my life were suffering. My three children were young and needed a father, and I knew that my wife, Sue, was carrying almost all the parenting burden.

Since my actuarial training was a way to leverage my success to a broader network of industry contacts, I'd begun volunteering on a variety of industry and professional boards and committees. I agreed to serve on a number of committees and task forces of the American Council of Life Insurance (ACLI), a trade association representing hundreds of insurance companies nationwide. Involvement with the ACLI enabled me to network with some of the top professionals in the insurance industry. While those contacts proved to be valuable, this level of industry service only exacerbated my work/life imbalance. I was away from the family even more and feeling even more guilty.

ACLI committee meetings were almost always held at its corporate offices in Washington, DC. Typically, I flew from Detroit to Washington the evening before an event, attended the meetings the next day, and returned to Detroit that evening... until one Thursday in May 1984, when this pattern fortuitously changed for the good.

It started ordinarily enough: Thursday afternoon, I flew into Washington for a Friday meeting of the Actuarial Committee. I checked in to my hotel near the Capitol, where someone recommended that I have dinner at the 1789, a historic restaurant in nearby Georgetown. After grabbing the documents I needed to read for Friday's meeting, I caught a cab to Georgetown. I was multitasking long before the word found its way into the popular jargon.

As usual, I watched the city go by through the windows of the cab, pondering the next day's meeting. It was a rainy, somewhat cold evening, but the restaurant was quaint and warm. The meal was wonderful, and the ambience was rustic but elegant. Since the dining room was too dark to read the documents I had brought along, I found myself intermittently deep in thought or observing others—in despair over my lack of productivity.

A few tables away was Bob Johannsen, a fellow member of the Actuarial Committee who would be attending the meeting with me the next morning. He was eating with a girl of about thirteen or fourteen. As I waited for my dessert to arrive, I began to worry about all the work I wasn't doing. But realizing the futility of this, I decided to shake it off and simply go say hello to Bob.

"Hi, Fred! So good to see you," said Bob warmly. "I'd like you to meet my daughter." Bob explained that he made a practice of bringing his children with him on business trips. "We stay an extra day or two to do some sightseeing."

I listened intently. They both looked so happy. What an excellent way for a busy executive to spend some quality time with his children. At the time, my daughters were nine-year-old Heidi, five-year-old Dena, and three-year-old Denise. Bob was just as busy as I was, but he'd found a way to add at least one element of balance to his life.

When I returned to the hotel, I immediately called my wife, Sue, and told her about Bob and his daughter. "What would you think of sending Heidi to Washington tomorrow? She and I could do some sightseeing over the weekend."

"That's a terrific idea!" said Sue. And she made the flight arrangements while I arranged for two more nights at the hotel.

I could hardly wait. After Friday's committee meeting, I rushed to the airport. At the age of nine, Heidi was understandably apprehensive about traveling alone for the first time, and I could see the nervousness on her face when she walked off the plane with her airline escort. But once she caught a glimpse of me, she broke into a broad smile. Not only was she relieved, but she was finally going to have some time alone with her dad.

I had been to Washington several times, but this was Heidi's first time. We planned two days of visiting major tourist sites: the Vietnam Memorial, the Washington Monument, the Lincoln Memorial, Arlington National Cemetery, and Ford's Theater, where Lincoln was assassinated. The weather was quite nice, so we did a lot of walking, and when we got to the Lincoln Memorial, Heidi begged me to race her up the steps.

"Here's an idea," I said, smiling. "How about if I stand here at the base and time *you* running up and down?"

Heidi thought this was a great challenge, and when she returned and I told her how long it had taken, she insisted—positively humming with unbounded youthful energy—on running it again in an attempt to beat her previous time. What fun!

At the Vietnam Memorial, I searched the Wall for the name of my junior high and high school friend, Arnie Sarna, who had been killed in the war. When I'd heard about the Vietnam Memorial, I was not particularly impressed with the design. But searching for Arnie's name and seeing hundreds of linear feet of personal notes, flowers, and memorabilia placed at the base of the Wall was something else—I couldn't move.

"Why are you crying, Daddy?" Heidi asked, turning to see what I was doing.

I struggled to explain the war and the loss of my friend to her, and suddenly I realized how moved Heidi was. This was important. This was good—for my daughter to share something so profound, for her to witness me reflecting on something so true and deep.

Here is another deep truth: when I'd boarded the plane for Washington the previous Thursday, I never could have imagined that a seemingly coincidental encounter with Bob Johannsen and his daughter would initiate a practice that would endure for the next twenty-five years—resulting in at least a hundred trips, impacting hundreds more people than my family (but I'll get to that in a minute).

Starting with that first trip with Heidi in 1984, I began taking each of my five children on annual trips alone with me for that special one-on-one bonding time. When the kids were young, a trip up the road to a local hotel for two or three nights was an exciting adventure. As they became teenagers and young adults, we sought out more educational and cultural experiences; the trips got more exotic and often included travel across the country, or even overseas. But in each case, the important thing was not where we traveled, but rather the fact that we did it together.

And this trip-taking practice birthed yet another practice: I would talk about this practice of taking trips with my children hundreds of times to thousands of New York Life employees and agents throughout my career—inspiring hundreds of those employees and agents to adopt the same practice with their own children.

Seeing how this single event impacted my career, my family, and my personal happiness, I now realize that God arranged that providential meeting at The 1789. I also recognize that God knew how the effects of it would ultimately play out over the ensuing years—multiplying the benefits exponentially as I shared our experiences. Even today, years after my retirement, the most frequent comment I receive in emails and holiday greeting cards from members of my extended family at New York Life is a thank-you for sharing the stories of those trips because so many of them adopted a similar practice with their own families.

During eight of the last eleven years of my career, New York Life achieved the number-one market share position in the sale of life insurance in the United States. We achieved many other distinctions and number-one rankings during those years, but I truly believe my greatest legacy to the company was more about my faith and my family values—values that inspired others—than any of those corporate achievements.

————————

If you have children at home, or if you plan to start a family soon, I sincerely hope you will consider implementing a similar practice to mine. I can assure you that you will be grateful you did, and you will be creating special memories for your children that will last a lifetime. If you are re-entering the workforce after a number of years of absence, your children may be grown, but consider implementing this technique with your grandchildren.

My Daily Balancing Routine

I am going to describe for you my daily routine, but I am not suggesting that you adopt the same practice. I did not realize until I retired from New York Life that I must have been seriously sleep-deprived throughout my career. Perhaps the Lord blessed me with a lesser need for sleep than most humans.

In any event, I hope you can modify the approach that I found useful and gratifying as appropriate to your situation.

Nearly every working day for me started by awakening at 4:00 a.m. It was such an engrained practice that I never needed to set an alarm clock.

Then I would proceed to my home workout area and mount my stationary bike for a forty-five-minute ride. A habitual multitasker, I would be on my Blackberry throughout that ride. Initially, I was doing nothing but New York Life work while on the exercise bike. I would typically read and answer emails, most of which had come in from the overseas operations of New York Life while I was sleeping.

After a couple of years of this routine, I decided I would use my morning time more effectively by communicating daily with my five children and my wife. I would write typically short emails (and later, short text messages) that simply checked in and asked how they were doing. I usually ended them with "I love you, and I am proud of you."

I didn't often receive responses unless I said, "Please acknowledge receipt of this message." Then I would get a two-word response: "Got it." But I knew they were reading my emails because if for some reason I missed a day or two, I would invariably get a message like this: "Hey Dad, what's up? No message today?"

Once I finished my bike ride, I would read a chapter from the Bible. When I first started this practice, I read from the Gospels of Matthew, Mark, Luke, and John. There is a total of ninety-nine chapters in the four Gospels, so I viewed this as my three-month start-up plan. If you start a practice like this (or any practice) and maintain it for three months, it becomes habit-forming and easy to sustain. I went on to focus on Proverbs and the Psalms, and eventually to all the books of the Bible.

After the Bible study, I went through my daily prayer list, which often contained more than two typed, single-spaced pages. I would list mostly intercessional prayers for others in need. I found this practice particularly gratifying because, over time, it was amazing how many of those prayers were answered. I highly recommend this practice. If I had to choose just one of these elements of my daily routine, it would be the prayer list.

By 6:00 a.m. every working day, before most people were even out of bed, I had accomplished a physical workout on the exercise bike, had communicated with my family through email or text messages, had heard from the Lord by reading His Word, and had spoken to the Lord in prayer. For me, it was an excellent way to start each day. I took comfort in knowing I did so as a way of balancing faith, family, and career.

Other Suggestions for Balancing Your Life

In numerous speaking engagements following the publication of my first two books, I would often try to generate spiritual sharing among the participants. Recognizing that many people find it difficult to muster the courage to share something deeply emotional, I would often start by telling them about my own coping techniques in attempting to better balance faith, family, and career.

I would then ask them if they had developed any of their own coping techniques. This was a relatively safe approach to triggering unemotional discussion and often led to strong engagement among the participants.

Below is a list of ideas that came out of those sessions for you to ponder in your own future efforts to achieve a better balance in your life:

- Family prayer time
- Family devotionals
- Dedicated one-on-one, face-to-face chat time with each child and/or your spouse
- A weekly date night with each child and/or your spouse
- Attendance at special events of interest to each child and your spouse
- Coaching of one of the kids' teams or one-on-one coaching of sports, music, or other activities of interest
- Attending special summer camps or events together
- Scheduled phone calls each day with each of the kids and your spouse
- Daily expressions of love—both verbal reminders and hugs

The list could be even longer. You might have techniques that aren't mentioned in this chapter. I strongly encourage you to make a regular habit of doing some of these things and stick to it until they become a normal routine part of your everyday activity. If you do, I am certain you and your family will benefit enormously from the commitment to spend more time together.

FINAL ADVICE: ENJOY THE JOURNEY

As I have stated elsewhere in this book, my passion (both pre- and post-retirement) has been to positively impact the lives of others in service to the Lord. Some readers of the early manuscript of this book suggested I split this into two books—one providing advice on following biblical principles in the workplace and the other on providing advice for fast-starting a career of consequence.

I strongly resisted those recommendations because I found the two topics not only to be a part of my DNA but inextricably linked in a symbiotic way that was a catalyst for rapid future personal growth, fulfillment, and happiness.

While I may have limited my audience of potential readers to some extent, I wanted to provide the most robust and meaningful advice I could give to those who chose to pick up this book and read it. I could not decouple the importance of my faith from the valuable experiences of my business career.

Like most people, I learned from my mistakes and was energized by my successes. By following the advice in this book, my hope and prayer is that you will avoid some of the mistakes I made and will enthusiastically embrace the action steps I am suggesting in the book. The workbook that supplements this book will enable you to track your progress relative to the many action steps suggested.

There is a lot of guidance provided in these chapters. Please don't be overwhelmed or discouraged by the task at hand. Many dozens of people (Christians and non-Christians alike) have already benefited enormously simply by following the five original tips I gave to my daughter, Dena, that are detailed in chapters 6 through 10.

You, your family, and your company will all benefit even more if you adhere to the biblical principles of Chapters 1 through 5 and if you systematically exercise the recommended advice in chapters 6 through 15.

You don't need to implement all of the recommendations immediately, nor should you attempt to do so. As I point out in several chapters, the timing of many of the action steps I suggest should occur as you mature in your new role and as you develop relevant on-the-job experiences. You will benefit even more if you develop a plan to proceed at a deliberate but realistically timed pace while using your unique spiritual gifts and remaining true to your values and beliefs.

Now, after my long and successful career in business, God has helped me find ways in which I can effectively touch more lives and make better use of my spiritual gifts. The exercise of writing this book has enabled me to meaningfully serve the Lord in a new and exciting way. I hope and pray that as you read this book, you will be inspired to embrace and implement its advice and, as a result, significantly enrich your future.

Congratulations on your entry or re-entry into the workplace! May the advice in this book result in a richly fulfilling career of consequence. Enjoy the journey!

"SPIRITUAL GIFTS IN THE MARKETPLACE" ASSESSMENT

In this appendix is a highly useful spiritual assessment created by Darren Shearer, founder of the Theology of Business Institute.

Darren began creating gift assessments that were "designed primarily to get people to volunteer at church on Sunday mornings." He says he created the *Spiritual Gifts in the Marketplace Assessment* specifically for Christian business professionals to help them understand that their spiritual gifts are applicable in the business world.

He has kindly provided permission for me to reprint his assessment here.[73]

Instructions

1. For each of the spiritual gift recognition statements, please rate yourself on a scale of 1 to 10 in the corresponding blanks on

the Response Sheet provided below (from page 87 of Darren's book): 1 = "Never," and 10 = "Always and without exception." You can download a blank copy of the Response Sheet at www. TheologyofBusiness.com/ResponseSheet.

2. For the most helpful results on this assessment:

- Spend no more than 20 seconds on each item. Go with your first instinct. Your immediate response is best.

- Remember that the goal is not to score high for any of the spiritual gift recognition statements. The goal is to have variances among your responses so you can identify your primary spiritual gifts.

- Be as honest with your answers as possible. This will produce the most helpful results.

Spiritual Gift Recognition Statements

1. "I organize ideas, resources, time, and people effectively."
2. "Ministry leaders look to me for guidance."
3. "People tell me I am a compassionate person."
4. "I like introducing people to each other."
5. "I enjoy creating and/or inventing new things and new ways of doing things."
6. "I am passionate about connecting with people from other cultures and nationalities."
7. "I have a unique ability to sense whether or not a person is acting in accordance with God's will."
8. "Through inspirational words, I often have helped people to think more optimistically about themselves and the world around them."
9. "I have challenged other Christians to share their faith with non-Christians."

10. "I have found it somewhat easy to believe God for things that seemed impossible to others."
11. "I regularly give money beyond my tithe toward the Lord's work."
12. "People often tell me I made them feel welcome in a new place."
13. "I am passionate about praying to God on behalf of others."
14. "I spend a significant percentage of my time learning new things."
15. "People often tell me I am a gifted leader."
16. "I am passionate about pursuing opportunities to see God work miracles wherever I go."
17. "I often take the time to care for the emotional and/or spiritual needs of people around me."
18. "I have communicated to others timely and urgent messages that I believe came directly from God."
19. "People around me know they can count on me to help out."
20. "I am passionate about putting in the extra effort to explain complicated concepts in a simple way so that people can understand."
21. "I often speak to God in an unknown, heavenly language."
22. "I apply the truth of God's Word in my everyday life."
23. "Others have told me I helped to lead them into the presence of God."
24. "People have told me I am a good planner and organizer."
25. "I have started multiple new ministries."
26. "My heart hurts when I see others hurting."
27. "I have connected many like-minded people together."
28. "People have told me I am a very creative person."
29. "I gravitate toward people who are from different cultures and nationalities than mine."

30. "Others have told me I have a special ability to perceive things most people are not able to perceive."

31. "I am passionate about motivating people to be more courageous."

32. "I am passionate about sharing the Gospel message with all types of people."

33. "People tell me I have a large amount of faith."

34. "Giving is one of my favorite things to do."

35. "I have invited guests into my home on a regular basis."

36. "People ask me to pray for them because they know I will actually pray."

37. "My life demonstrates that I am passionate about learning new things."

38. "I prefer to focus on the bigger picture while other people work on the details."

39. "When people need a miracle to happen in their lives, such as a healing miracle, they often ask me to pray for them."

40. "I am passionate about connecting with, caring for, and coaching others one-on-one."

41. "I don't mind confronting people about their faulty thinking."

42. "I enjoy doing the tasks my leaders don't have time to do."

43. "I teach everywhere I go…not just in a classroom setting."

44. "To strengthen myself spiritually, I speak to my spirit regularly in an unknown, heavenly language."

45. "I intuitively find solutions to complicated problems."

46. "Throughout the day, I am keenly aware of the presence, majesty, and goodness of God."

47. "I enjoy figuring out what needs to get done to accomplish larger objectives."

48. "God tends to place me before influential people to represent Him and His Kingdom."

49. "I am passionate about helping to alleviate people's sufferings."
50. "People have told me I am good at networking."
51. "I have created many new things and/or new ways of doing things."
52. "People have told me I should be a missionary in another culture."
53. "I believe I have a special responsibility to sense when situations are spiritually unhealthy."
54. "People have told me they feel encouraged when they are around me."
55. "I have led many people to Jesus during my lifetime."
56. "I am passionate about trusting God to do big things."
57. "People who know me well would say I am a generous person."
58. "I am passionate about helping strangers to feel welcome when they are in my presence."
59. "I pray for extended amounts of time concerning the needs in our world."
60. "People view me as a source of information."
61. "I am passionate about getting other people involved and leveraging their unique abilities to accomplish large objectives."
62. "I have prayed for specific miracles, signs, wonders, and healings to happen and have seen many of them come to pass."
63. "People often share their personal struggles with me because they trust me."
64. "Other people have confirmed that they believe I speak God's truth about specific situations."
65. "I am eager to help even when others are not."
66. "People have told me I am a good teacher."
67. "I have spoken a message from God to others in an unknown, heavenly language that I or someone else interpreted."
68. "People often ask me how to deal with confusing situations."

69. "I set apart time every day to worship God and invite His presence into my life and into the atmosphere around me wherever I go."

You can download a blank PDF copy of this response sheet at www. TheologyofBusiness.com/ResponseSheet. It contains space to write your self-assessment for each of the sixty-nine questions, along with space to write your total point counts.

Response Sheet   **Totals**

1. ____	24. ____	47. ____	A.____
2. ____	25. ____	48. ____	B.____
3. ____	26. ____	49. ____	C.____
4. ____	27. ____	50. ____	D.____
5. ____	28. ____	51. ____	E.____
6. ____	29. ____	52. ____	F.____
7. ____	30. ____	53. ____	G.____
8. ____	31. ____	54. ____	H.____
9. ____	32. ____	55. ____	I.____
10. ____	33. ____	56. ____	J.____
11. ____	34. ____	57. ____	K.____
12. ____	35. ____	58. ____	L.____
13. ____	36. ____	59. ____	M.____
14. ____	37. ____	60. ____	N.____
15. ____	38. ____	61. ____	O.____
16. ____	39. ____	62. ____	P.____
17. ____	40. ____	63. ____	Q.____
18. ____	41. ____	64. ____	R.____
19. ____	42. ____	65. ____	S.____
20. ____	43. ____	66. ____	T.____
21. ____	44. ____	67. ____	U.____
22. ____	45. ____	68. ____	V.____
23. ____	46. ____	69. ____	W.____

Calculating the Results

For each line on the "Response Sheet," add the three numbers across for each letter, and write the totals next to each corresponding letter. (For example, your responses for #1 plus #24 plus #47 would add up to the amount you would place in the blank for "A," which is the gift of administration.) Then write in the corresponding spiritual gifts and circle your top three or four highest-scoring spiritual gifts.

A = Administration
B = Apostleship
C = Compassion
D = Connecting
E = Creativity
F = Cross-Cultural Ministry
G = Discernment
H = Encouragement
I = Evangelism
J = Faith
K = Giving
L = Hospitality
M = Intercessory Prayer
N = Knowledge
O = Leadership
P = Miracle-Working & Healing
Q = Pastoring
R = Prophecy
S = Service
T = Teaching
U = Tongues & Interpretation
V = Wisdom
W = WorshipDefinitions and Examples

Refer to the following links for definitions of each spiritual gift, as well as an example of how each gift has been used in a business setting. The gifts correspond to lines A–W on the prior page.

(A) Administration:
www.TheologyofBusiness.com/GiftOfAdministration
(B) Apostleship:
www.TheologyofBusiness.com/GiftOfApostleship
(C) Compassion:
www.TheologyofBusiness.com/GiftOfCompassion
(D) Connecting:
www.TheologyofBusiness.com/GiftOfConnecting
(E) Creativity:
www.TheologyofBusiness.com/GiftOfCreativity
(F) Cross-Cultural Ministry:
www.TheologyofBusiness.com/GiftOfCrossCulturalMinistry
(G) Discernment:
www.TheologyofBusiness.com/GiftOfDiscernment
(H) Encouragement:
www.TheologyofBusiness.com/GiftOfEncouragement
(I) Evangelism:
www.TheologyofBusiness.com/GiftOfEvangelism
(J) Faith:
www.TheologyofBusiness.com/GiftOfFaith
(K) Giving:
www.TheologyofBusiness.com/GiftOfGiving
(L) Hospitality:
www.TheologyofBusiness.com/GiftOfHospitality
(M) Intercessory Prayer:
www.TheologyofBusiness.com/GiftOfIntercessoryPrayer

(N) Knowledge:

www.TheologyofBusiness.com/GiftOfKnowledge

(O) Leadership:

www.TheologyofBusiness.com/GiftOfLeadership

(P) Miracle-Working & Healing:

www.TheologyofBusiness.com/GiftsOfMiraclesAndHealing

(Q) Pastoring:

www.TheologyofBusiness.com/GiftOfPastoring

(R) Prophecy:

www.TheologyofBusiness.com/GiftOfProphecy

(S) Service:

www.TheologyofBusiness.com/GiftOfService

(T) Teaching:

www.TheologyofBusiness.com/GiftOfTeaching

(U) Tongues & Interpretation:

www.TheologyofBusiness.com/GiftsOfTonguesAndInterpretation

(V) Wisdom:

www.TheologyofBusiness.com/GiftOfWisdom

(W) Worship:

www.TheologyofBusiness.com/GiftOfWorship

APPENDIX B

WHAT YOU CAN LEARN FROM THE BIBLE AND JESUS ABOUT LEADING AND MANAGING

Not everyone aspires to be a leader or manager, nor does everyone have the spiritual gifts associated with leadership or management. However, if you do have those gifts and you do aspire to take on more leadership or management responsibilities, the information in this appendix can provide valuable guidance and insights.

Learning from Jesus

The behaviors and the words of Jesus can set an example for you and be quite uplifting and informative throughout your career. Understanding the ways in which Jesus conducted Himself while in human form are worthy of emulation. They can greatly impact your future, whether you are an entrepreneur starting your own business, a high-level executive in a larger organization, a mid-level manager, or an entry-level employee.

The most important thing Jesus told us that you need to remember is that He will be with us always and that He will give us an advocate in the form of the Holy Spirit.

You can take great comfort in the promises He made to us in the following Scriptures from the firsthand witnesses and authors of the four Gospels. There are dozens of verses that reinforce the statements below, but I chose to quote just one of my favorites from each of the four Gospels.

Jesus assures us of his dominion and his eternal presence:

"Then Jesus came to them and said, 'All authority in heaven and on earth has been given to me. Therefore, go and make disciples of all nations, baptizing them in the name of the Father and of the Son and of the Holy Spirit, and teaching them to obey everything I have commanded you. And surely, I am with you always, to the very end of the age.'"
—Matthew 28:18–20

Jesus tells us that with God, all things are possible:

"Jesus looked at them and said, 'With man this is impossible, but not with God; all things are possible with God.'"
—Mark 10:27

Jesus assures us of the power of prayer:

"So I say to you: Ask and it will be given to you; seek and you will find; knock and the door will be opened to you. For everyone who

asks receives; the one who seeks finds; and to the one who knocks, the door will be opened."

—Luke 11:9–10

Jesus promises that the Holy Spirit will be given to those who keep His commands:

"If you love me, keep my commands. And I will ask the Father, and he will give you another advocate to help you and be with you forever."

—John 14:15–16

What Jesus Says about Work

Although many of the verses below don't address workplace matters directly, they are words Jesus spoke that, as a Christian, you need to be mindful of in your work life.

Your primary objective in the workplace should be to serve the Lord, not to amass wealth:

"What good is it for someone to gain the whole world, yet forfeit their soul? Or what can anyone give in exchange for their soul?"

—Mark 8:36

If your priorities are well-aligned with Jesus's teachings, you will be rewarded:

"But seek first his kingdom and his righteousness, and all these things will be given to you as well."

—Matthew 6:33

As you face difficult issues and challenges in the workplace, rely on faith:

> *"He replied, 'Because you have so little faith. Truly I tell you, if you have faith as small as a mustard seed, you can say to this mountain, "Move from here to there," and it will move. Nothing will be impossible for you.'"*
> —Matthew 17:20

Jesus wants to see you thrive and grow:

> *"His master replied, 'Well done, good and faithful servant! You have been faithful with a few things; I will put you in charge of many things. Come and share your master's happiness!'"*
> —Matthew 25:23

Don't restrict your prayer life only to Sundays or only to your house of worship. Pray often at work:

> *"Therefore I tell you, whatever you ask for in prayer, believe that you have received it, and it will be yours."*
> —Mark 11:24

Earn trust through honesty and integrity:

> *"Whoever can be trusted with very little can also be trusted with much, and whoever is dishonest with very little will also be dishonest with much."*
> —Luke 16:10

Emulating Jesus as a Leader and Manager

Libraries, bookstores, and online retailers have hundreds of books on leadership and on management. Listing all the qualities of good managers and leaders would be a daunting task. What follows is just a partial list of the many qualities that Jesus possessed. Many of those qualities are revealed in the Gospels and elsewhere in the New Testament.

The evidence in Scripture supports the following statements concerning Jesus that reveal much about the source of His effectiveness as a leader and manager of people. These same qualities and characteristics can enable you to better emulate Jesus and become a much more effective partner with Him in your career advancement and development.

As you read about Jesus's leadership and management qualities and behaviors, ask yourself where you fall short of His example. Make notes of how you can improve in those areas.

Jesus's Demeanor and Treatment of Others

The following are traits of Jesus that are revealed in many New Testament passages. I have chosen one representative passage as an example for each trait.

Jesus often demonstrates his compassion:

"And a leper came to him, imploring him, and kneeling said to him, 'If you will, you can make me clean.' Moved with pity, he stretched out his hand and touched him and said to him, 'I will; be clean.' And immediately the leprosy left him, and he was made clean."

—Mark 1:41–42 (ESV)

Jesus exhibits a toughness in dealing with adversaries:

"Woe to you, teachers of the law and Pharisees, you hypocrites! You shut the door of the kingdom of heaven in people's faces. You yourselves do not enter, nor will you let those enter who are trying to. Woe to you, teachers of the law and Pharisees, you hypocrites!"
—Matthew 23:13–15

Jesus expresses anger appropriately:

"Jesus entered the temple courts and drove out all who were buying and selling there. He overturned the tables of the money changer and the benches of those selling doves. 'It is written,' he said to them, 'My house will be called a house of prayer,' but you are making it a den of robbers.'"
—Matthew 21:12–13

Jesus loves people and understands the importance of personal relationships:

"My command is this: Love each other as I have loved you. Greater love has no one than this: to lay down one's life for one's friends. You are my friends if you do what I command. I no longer call you servants, because a servant does not know his master's business. Instead, I have called you friends, for everything that I learned from my Father I have made known to you."
—John 15:12–15

Jesus believes in people who often don't believe in themselves:

"Jesus entered Jericho and was passing through. A man was there by the name of Zacchaeus; he was a chief tax collector and was wealthy. He wanted to see who Jesus was, but because he was short he could

not see over the crowd. So he ran ahead and climbed a sycamore-fig tree to see him, since Jesus was coming that way. When Jesus reached the spot, he looked up and said to him, 'Zacchaeus, come down immediately. I must stay at your house today.' So he came down at once and welcomed him gladly. All the people saw this and began to mutter, 'He has gone to be the guest of a sinner.' But Zacchaeus stood up and said to the Lord, 'Look, Lord! Here and now I give half of my possessions to the poor, and if I have cheated anybody out of anything, I will pay back four times the amount."

—Luke 19:1–8

Jesus perseveres and endures difficult times:

"From that time on Jesus began to explain to his disciples that he must go to Jerusalem and suffer many things at the hands of the elders, the chief priests and the teachers of the law, and that he must be killed and on the third day be raised to life."

—Matthew 16:21

Jesus has great self-awareness:

"I and the Father are one."

—John 10:30

Jesus as a Manager

Jesus also exhibits strong management skills, particularly in how He handles apostles and disciples.

Jesus coaches and develops His team:

"Aware of their discussion, Jesus asked, 'You of little faith, why are you talking among yourselves about having no bread? Do you still

not understand? Don't you remember the five loaves for the five thousand, and how many basketfuls you gathered? Or the seven loaves for the four thousand, and how many basketfuls you gathered? How is it you don't understand that I was not talking to you about bread? But be on your guard against the yeast of the Pharisees and Sadducees.' Then they understood that he was not telling them to guard against the yeast used in bread, but against the teaching of the Pharisees and Sadducees."

—Matthew 16:8–12

Jesus praises:

"When Jesus saw Nathanael approaching, he said of him, 'Here truly is an Israelite in whom there is no deceit.'"

—John 1:47

Jesus rebukes:

"Peter took him aside and began to rebuke him. 'Never, Lord!' he said. 'This shall never happen to you!' Jesus turned and said to Peter, 'Get behind me, Satan! You are a stumbling block to me; you do not have in mind the concerns of God, but merely human concerns.'"

—Matthew 16:22–23

Jesus sets lofty goals:

"After this the Lord appointed seventy-two others and sent them two by two ahead of him to every town and place where he was about to go. He told them, 'The harvest is plentiful, but the workers are few.

Ask the Lord of the harvest, therefore, to send out workers into his harvest field. Go! I am sending you out like lambs among wolves.'"
—Luke 10:1–4

Jesus delegates effectively:

"When Jesus had called the Twelve together, he gave them power and authority to drive out all demons and to cure diseases, and he sent them out to proclaim the kingdom of God and to heal the sick."
—Luke 9:1–2

Jesus as a Leader

Jesus sets an example for us on how to be an effective leader. Jesus is visionary, He has long-term objectives:

"Then Jesus came to them and said, 'All authority in heaven and on earth has been given to me. Therefore go and make disciples of all nations, baptizing them in the name of the Father and of the Son and of the Holy Spirit, and teaching them to obey everything I have commanded you. And surely I am with you always, to the very end of the age.'"
—Matthew 16:18–20

Jesus passes the litmus test of leadership in that "they will follow":

"'Come, follow me,' Jesus said, 'and I will send you out to fish for people.' At once they left their nets and followed him.'"
—Mark 1:17

Jesus is a great storyteller (largely in parables):

"Or suppose a woman has ten silver coins and loses one. Doesn't she light a lamp, sweep the house and search carefully until she finds it? And when she finds it, she calls her friends and neighbors together and says, 'Rejoice with me; I have found my lost coin.' In the same way, I tell you, there is rejoicing in the presence of the angels of God over one sinner who repents."

—Luke 15:8–10

Jesus doesn't compromise on the most important matters:

"Jesus answered him, 'It is also written: "Do not put the Lord your God to the test." Again, the devil took him to a very high mountain and showed him all the kingdoms of the world and their splendor. 'All this I will give you,' he said, 'if you will bow down and worship me.' Jesus said to him, 'Away from me, Satan! For it is written: "Worship the Lord your God, and serve him only."'"

—Matthew 4:7–10

On a daily basis, share your workplace challenges and issues with Him and ask for guidance.

Remember, the most important thing Jesus told us is that He will be with us always and that He will give us an advocate in the form of the Holy Spirit. You can take great comfort in the promises He made to us in Scripture, as demonstrated above. So be sure to keep Jesus close as you deal with challenges in leadership and management, both small and large. You will feel the presence of the Holy Spirit!

APPENDIX C
THE AUTHOR'S FAITH JOURNEY

Every life is a unique journey. Mine began like that of millions of other Americans, in an unremarkable and very typical lower-middle-income household. I was born to second- and third-generation European immigrants who worked hard to support and sustain a young family in a rebounding post-World War II economy.

Throughout my childhood, my parents struggled financially. Neither my mother nor my father graduated from high school. They were Depression-era teenagers forced to work to support their families; that work ethic persisted for the rest of their lives.

I took only one short vacation as a child and didn't fly in an airplane until I left home for college. As a result, the formation of my attitude toward money, work, and sacrifice was shaped in ways unlike those of other kids whose parents were much more comfortable financially. For me, pursuit of the American Dream was an early and driving ambition.

My father worked long, hard hours as an insurance inspector. A working-class guy who collected data for low pay, he supplemented his income by following his real passion: playing the trumpet. It was his passion for music—not his work in the insurance industry—that defined him and his life.

His dedication to his passion affected my childhood and my adult life as I identified and pursued my own passions. Even now, I think of Dad's overarching passion when I tell people that my own passion is to serve the Lord by using my spiritual gifts to positively impact the lives of others in ways that reflect both my faith and my business experience.

It's been said that if you follow your passions, you'll never work a day in your life. For me, this couldn't be truer. For many decades, I have been blessed and spiritually enriched because there has been total harmony in my love for the Lord, my eagerness to serve Him, and my pursuit of ways to use my spiritual gifts during my working lifetime and thereafter.

Raised by Non-Worshipping, but Good and Loving Working-Class Parents

Dad had a strong faith in God but rarely expressed it and did not regularly take the family to church. It was difficult for him to express the things he felt strongly about; he rarely revealed emotions to his family. But as I watched him handle life's challenges, I came to understand the depth of his faith.

Mom didn't often express her faith, either. But she was less guarded with her emotions and did find occasions to express her faith in God and her reliance on His direction and guidance. She, too, worked several low-paying jobs and enjoyed being engaged in something productive. She was a lifetime learner, eager to advance her knowledge, even as she became fragile and forgetful in her early eighties.

I am forever grateful that I was raised by good and loving working-class parents who instilled in me moral values and an awareness of biblical principles. However, unlike most strong Christian families, we did not regularly attend worship services.

Although it may sound odd, I think my lack of formal religious training as a child had both a negative and a positive impact on the future development of my faith.

On the negative side, I did not affiliate at a young age with any particular body of believers. Unlike many children in Christian families, I did not learn Bible stories, with their inherent wisdom and moralistic values. And I did not have the benefit of worshipping and interacting regularly with other believers.

But there were positive aspects to this background as well. I was not indoctrinated into a narrowly defined religious belief system. I was inspired to pursue my beliefs independently, with an open mind while I contemplated and considered many difficult theological questions. And God knew I needed divine revelation to fortify my faith.

Kitchen-Table Chats about Integrity

It was through numerous kitchen-table chats with Mom that I gained enhanced self-worth and self-confidence. Ironically, although God or religion didn't come up often in those discussions, a lot of moral principles did, and they became embedded in my psyche. Mom always encouraged me to work hard and to do so with integrity. She always emphasized doing what was right. Our chats may not have been formal Bible studies, but Mom often quoted the Ten Commandments and the Golden Rule as principles by which I should live my life. I listened and absorbed what she was saying. I believed her.

Even in the competitive, secular corporate world, I always did my best to follow my mother's advice. I worked hard, striving to demonstrate integrity while being ever-mindful of compassion and the

Ten Commandments. Ever since the early days of my career, because of my strong faith, I had no hesitation in expressing that faith and speaking of my relationship with the Lord.

Those extremely simple instructions from my parents and their demonstration of how to live accordingly have stayed with me for a lifetime. Those early experiences ultimately led me on a journey to find Jesus Christ. What a blessing it is to have had childhood experiences that were so positive.

I believe my testimony today is even more powerful because I chose to follow Jesus—not because doing so was instilled in me as a child, but rather because I came to know Him, believe in Him, and commit my life to Him while I simultaneously pursued a successful career in business.

Theological Questions Led Me to Seek the Lord

So how did I come to know the Lord?

Those early childhood experiences with my parents piqued my curiosity about God and religion. They caused me to ask questions of friends and acquaintances who attended church more regularly than I did. But I always ended up with more questions than answers, and the multitude of faiths practiced in my own small neighborhood often resulted in conflicting answers from different sources. It all seemed very confusing and complicated.

If I chose to follow a single faith tradition or denomination, I'd get only one perspective and miss all the others. How would I know which was right? On the other hand, if I pursued answers from every possible source, I would continue to be confused and wonder if any of it made sense. I didn't think I was posing deep theological questions. I was just a young kid who wanted to know if God was real, if He existed now or only in the past, and if He could hear and would answer my prayers.

I had other questions. Did God know who I was? Was He watching over my every move and protecting me? Were there really angels?

I also wondered a lot about Jesus and what it meant to be the Son of God. How could God be a single divine being, yet be in three forms (God the Father, Jesus the Son, and the Holy Spirit)—the Holy Trinity?

When people said God spoke to them, were they lying or delusional? Did God really speak audibly? Why couldn't *I* hear God?

And why did so many bad things happen in the world—often to such good people? My list of questions seemed endless.

This series of questions and musings ultimately led to the pivotal spiritual event of my life that I described as a mystical adolescent experience more fully in chapter 1 of this book.

Simple questions like these eventually proved to be deeply theological after all. I didn't have good answers then, and I don't have good answers to all of them now, even after four years of divinity school studies. But during my lifetime, God's unconditional love has been revealed to me, especially through the gift and sacrifice of His son Jesus Christ. And as I continue to read and reflect daily on Bible passages, I extract value and learn more about the nature, goodness, and grace of a loving, omnipresent God.

Sharing My Faith with Others

My passion has always been to positively impact people's lives. Seven years of teaching junior high school after graduating from Amherst College in 1970 was an early and gratifying fulfillment of that passion.

Then, as I entered the insurance profession, I felt equally fulfilled as I learned of millions of families being saved from financial ruin, following the untimely death or disability of the family's primary wage-earner, because they had purchased life or disability insurance.

I was often moved to tears by the stories of how a young widower or widow grieving the loss of a spouse was greatly comforted knowing his or her mortgage was paid for and the children's education was funded by life or disability insurance proceeds. Nothing could be more devastating, at a time of extreme grief, than to be forced to sell one's primary residence and not knowing how to fund the children's higher education.

When I retired from the New York Life Insurance Company, the company was paying more than three hundred death claims per day, exceeding $3 billion in benefits per year to grieving families in need. This indeed was a blessing to me; it was reassurance that I was using my spiritual gifts to serve the Lord in my chosen vocation. It was an added fulfillment of my passion to positively impact people's lives.

After that long and rewarding career, I retired as the president of the company at age fifty-nine to attend divinity school at Yale University and fulfill my long-time dream of devoting dedicated time to greatly enhance my spiritual education and development.

On my first day of divinity school, as I left my home in Connecticut carrying my book bag and heading to New Haven, my adult daughter, Heidi, was visiting us. She yelled out from the family room, "Play nice with the other kids, and don't forget to share!" As funny as that was to hear, it actually was quite profound.

The divinity school experience for me was all about sharing my faith with others. That realization ultimately led me to new ways to pursue my passion of positively impacting people's lives in ways I had never anticipated. But it wasn't new for me because I had been sharing my faith in the workplace for decades.

How many people say to themselves daily, "I am really happy right now"? I was acutely aware of that happiness every day of the four years during which I sat in classrooms and interacted with professors, administrators, and other students at Yale Divinity School. Even though I was older and far more conservative (both theologically and politically) than most at Yale, I truly loved the experience and felt totally unconstrained in expressing my evangelical perspective.

I went on to write two faith-based books that have positively impacted thousands of readers and thousands of others through TV and radio appearances, as well as personal appearances in churches, Bible-study classes, small discussion groups, and in keynote presentations to larger gatherings of Christians.

While still in divinity school, I started to write my first book (*God Revealed: Revisit Your Past to Enrich Your Future*), which recounts thirty-one stories about my own encounters with God over the course of my life. As the subtitle suggests, the stories and the reflection questions following each story were designed to serve as memory triggers for readers of their own encounters with God. After reading stories in the book, a significant number of readers reported that the stories and the reflection questions indeed triggered memories of experiences that they had not previously considered providential.

After writing and promoting the first book, I often told people I viewed my long business career as mere prologue to what I was doing in retirement: speaking and writing about my faith.

In 2013, I was asked to write an article about retirement for *Wealth Channel Magazine*. My article, "Happier, Healthier, and Younger in Retirement," was published that year. That's exactly how I felt then and how I feel now. When you are following your passion and God's calling for your life, you can't help feeling happier, healthier, and younger.

In my numerous speaking engagements after writing the first book, I met a great number of interesting and faithful people who shared with me their stories of overcoming severe crises. Again, the power of spiritual sharing was evident as my stories encouraged others and gave them permission to tell me their stories.

My second book, *Grace Revealed: Finding God's Strength in Any Crisis*, tells the compelling stories of nineteen people who had experienced extreme crises and recovered only by the grace of God and through their faith in, and relationship with, Jesus Christ.

For that book, I hired a researcher to provide information on the prevalence of the crises covered in each chapter of the book so readers would be reassured that they were not alone. There are multiple stories within chapters on topics including sexual and emotional abuse, addictions, depression, PTSD, and the loss of a loved one.

This third book (*Fast-Starting a Career of Consequence: Practical Christ-Centered Advice for Entering or Re-Entering the Workforce*) is yet another fulfillment of my passion and a response to God's calling.

ABOUT THE AUTHOR

After earning a bachelor's degree from Amherst College and a master's degree in statistics from Wayne State University, Frederick J. Sievert began his career as a junior high school mathematics teacher. He later entered the insurance business as an actuarial trainee. After a rapid rise to the top of the organization, with responsibility for 65,000 agents and employees worldwide, he ultimately retired in 2007 as president of the New York Life Insurance Company, a Fortune 100 corporation.

Following his early retirement at age fifty-nine, Sievert attended Yale Divinity School to enhance the spiritual development and education he felt he had neglected during his successful but intense career. He was awarded a master's degree in religion from Yale in 2011.

In retirement, Sievert is following his passion to serve the Lord by using his spiritual gifts to positively impact the lives of others in ways that reflect both his faith and his business experience.

In addition, he remains actively engaged in writing, teaching, mentoring young executives, serving on the boards of five nonprofit organizations and two for-profit corporations, and following his calling into the ministry created by his first book, *God Revealed: Revisit Your Past to Enrich Your Future*. His second book, *Grace Revealed: Finding God's Strength in Any Crisis*, recounts stories of people in severe crises who found relief and recovery through their faith and personal relationships with Christ.

Sievert has been in leadership roles in all the churches he has attended since he was in his twenties.

A frequent speaker, Sievert addresses audiences ranging in size from small book clubs and Bible-study classes to large national conventions. He has completed more than fifty TV and radio interviews, which include appearances on Fox & Friends, the Fox Business Channel, and the Daystar Christian network. Two of the stories from his second book were featured as videos on *The 700 Club* in May 2019.

ENDNOTES

1   Arthur F. Miller, Jr., and Bill Hendricks, *The Power of Uniqueness: How to Become Who You Really Are* (Grand Rapids, Michigan: Zondervan, 2002), 223.

2   Ibid., 106.

3   Ibid., 106–107. Note that I have added the parenthetical Scripture references to indicate passages in the Bible that attest to the statements Miller has made.

4   Ibid., 107.

5   "9 Things You Should Know About the Apostles' Creed," Joe Carter, The Gospel Coalition (TGC), December 12, 2018, https://www.thegospelcoalition.org/article/9-things-know-apostles-creed/.

6   "5 Companies with Values That Stand Above the Rest," Thomas Wachtel, Element Three, March 13, 2020, https://elementthree.com/blog/5-examples-of-companies-with-awesome-core-values/.

7   "Our Story," Hobby Lobby website, https://newsroom.
    hobbylobby.com/corporate-background/.

8   "18 Extremely Religious Big American Companies, Max Nisen,
    Business Insider, June 13, 2013, https://www.businessinsider.
    com/18-extremely-religious-big-american-companies-2013-6.

9   "Support/Corporate Employment," In-N-Out Burger website,
    https://www.in-n-out.com/employment/corporate/home.

10 "Core Values: Overview and Examples," Indeed.com, April 2,
    2020, https://www.indeed.com/career-advice/career-development/
    core-values.

11 "Top Ten Work Values Employers Look For," Penny Loretto,
    The Balance Careers, updated November 24, 2019, https://
    www.thebalancecareers.com/top-work-values-employers-look-
    for-1986763.

12 "The Personality Traits That Will Get You Hired," Katharine
    Paljug, *Business News Daily*, February 9, 2018, https://www.
    businessnewsdaily.com/7950-personality-traits-hired.html.

13 "What Does the Bible Say about Christian Values and
    Christian Life?" Christian Bible Reference Site, https://www.
    christianbiblereference.org/faq_ChristianValues.htm.

14 "Bandwidth CEO Relies on a Higher Calling to Build Raleigh
    Firm into $2B Success," Faith-Driven Entrepreneur, September 11,
    2019, https://www.faithdrivenentrepreneur.org/blog/2019/9/11/
    bandwidth-ceo-relies-on-a-higher-calling-to-build-raleigh-firm-
    into-2b-success.

15 "Chiefs' Christ-Following Culture Starts at the Top with CEO/
    Owner Clark Hunt," Jon Ackerman, Sports Spectrum, January
    31, 2020, https://sportsspectrum.com/sport/football/2020/01/31/
    chiefs-christ-following-culture-starts-with-ceo-owner-clark-hunt/.

16 "High-Profile Christian Business Leaders," Tim Parker,
    Investopedia, updated October 5, 2018, https://www.investopedia.

com/financial-edge/0912/high-profile-christian-business-leaders. aspx; and "18 Extremely Religious Big American Companies," Max Nisen, Business Insider, June 13, 2013, https://www. businessinsider.com/18-extremely-religious-big-american-companies-2013-6#tyson-foods-employs-1290-office-chaplains-to-provide-compassionate-pastoral-care-to-employees-3.

17   "10 Companies You Probably Didn't Know Were Christian Owned," The Praying Woman, https://theprayingwoman.com/10-companies-you-probably-didnt-know-were-christian-owned/.

18   "Success Tips from 5 CEOs with Humble Beginnings, Chantal Bechervaise, Take Personelly, April 21, 2017, https:// takeitpersonelly.com/2017/04/21/success-tips-from-5-ceos-with-humble-beginnings/,

19   "Truett Cathy Lived a Life Centered on Family," Dick Parker, The Chicken Wire, August 11, 2016, https://thechickenwire.chick-fil-a.com/inside-chick-fil-a/a-life-centered-on-family.

20   Ibid.

21   "The Effects of Prayer on Attention Resource Availability and Attention Bias," Holly Adams, Heather M. Kleider-Offutt, David Bell, and David A. Washburn, *Religion, Brain & Behavior* 7, no. 2 (2017): 117–33, https://www.tandfonline.com/doi/abs/10.1080/2153599X.2016.1206612?journalCode=rrbb20&.

22   "Unlocking the Power of Prayer," Elizabeth Lombardo, *Success*, December 30, 2017, https://www.success.com/unlocking-the-power-of-prayer/.

23   "New Study Examines the Effects of Prayer on Mental Health," Traci Pedersen, Psych Central, updated July 8, 2018, https:// psychcentral.com/blog/new-study-examines-the-effects-of-prayer-on-mental-health/.

24   "Prayer and Satisfaction with Sacrifice in Close Relationships," Nathaniel M. Lambert, Frank D. Fincham, and Scott

Stanley, *Journal of Social and Personal Relationships 29*, no. 8 (2012): 1058–70, https://journals.sagepub.com/doi/abs/10.1177/0265407512449316.

25 "What Prayer Is Good For—And the Evidence for It," Clay Routledge, *National Review*, April 9, 2018, https://www.nationalreview.com/2018/04/what-prayer-is-good-for-and-the-evidence-for-it/.

26 "Religious Involvement, Spirituality, and Medicine: Implications for Clinical Practice," Paul S. Mueller, MD; David J. Plevak, MD; and Teresa A. Rummans, MD, *Mayo Clinic Proceedings 76* (December 2001): 1225–35, https://www.mayoclinicproceedings.org/article/S0025-6196(11)62799-7/pdf.

27 "Why Commitment Is the New Must-Have Quality for Employees," David Hassell, 15Five.com, undated, https://www.15five.com/blog/why-commitment-is-the-new-must-have-quality-for-employees/.

28 Ibid.

29 "The Six Traits High-Performing Employees Share," Ankit Patel, *Forbes*, May 21, 2019, https://www.forbes.com/sites/theyec/2019/05/21/the-six-traits-high-performing-employees-share/#22b8c54416fb. The Forbes Young Entrepreneur Council (YEC) is an invitation-only, fee-based organization comprised of the world's most successful entrepreneurs who are forty-five and younger.

30 "When Under Stress, Managers Reveal Their Dark Sides," Dana Wilkie, Society for Human Resource Management, December 12, 2018, https://www.shrm.org/resourcesandtools/hr-topics/employee-relations/pages/dark-side-of-bosses-under-stress.aspx.

31 Ibid.

32 "Few Employees Believe in Their Company's Values," Nate Dvorak and Bailey Nelson, Gallup, September 13, 2016, https://news.

gallup.com/businessjournal/195491/few-employees-believe-company-values.aspx.

33 "Mission & Vision Statements: What Is the Difference?" March 5, 2018, Society for Human Resource Management, https://login. shrm.org/?request_id=id2D8D14DC02E599&relay_state=id-bc8b2c99-d3dc-49a0-9502-bc333a87915c&issuer=aHR0cHM6 Ly9zc28uc2hybS5vcmcvSURCVVMvU0hSTS9JRFAvU0FNTDIv TUQ=&target=aHR0cHM6Ly9zc28uc2hybS5vcmcvSURCVV MvU0hSTS9QT1JUQUwtU1AvU0FNTDIvTUQ=.

34 "Difference between Vision and Mission Statements: 25 Examples," Brett Skrabanek, ClearVoice, August 19, 2018, https:// www.clearvoice.com/blog/difference-between-mission-vision-statement-examples/.

35 "5 Reasons Why Mission-Driven Leaders Are the Most Successful," Marie-Claire Ross, LinkedIn, December 14, 2015, https://www. linkedin.com/pulse/5-reasons-why-mission-driven-leaders-most-successful-ross-gaicd.

36 "Millennials Are the Largest Generation in the US Labor Force," Richard Fry, Pew Research Center, April 11, 2018, https:// www.pewresearch.org/fact-tank/2018/04/11/millennials-largest-generation-us-labor-force/.

37 "Workplace Culture Trends: The Key to Hiring (and Keeping) Top Talent in 2019," Nina McQueen, LinkedIn, June 26, 2018, https://blog.linkedin.com/2018/june/26/workplace-culture-trends-the-key-to-hiring-and-keeping-top-talent.

38 "Defining Company Culture: It's about Business Performance, Not Free Meals and Game Rooms," Natalie Baumgartner, *Forbes*, January 15, 2019, https://www.forbes.com/sites/ forbeshumanresourcescouncil/2019/01/15/defining-company-culture-its-about-business-performance-not-free-meals-and-game-rooms/#3024a1321e9d.

39 "Workers Value a Strong Company Culture over Higher Pay, Study Claims," Chloe Taylor, CNBC, July 11, 2019, https://www. cnbc.com/2019/07/11/workers-value-a-strong-company-culture-over-higher-pay-study-claims.html.

40 Ibid.

41 "Build a Culture That Increases Employee Retention," Matt D'Angelo, *Business News Daily*, updated May 9, 2018, https:// www.businessnewsdaily.com/8718-attracting-retaining-strategies. html.

42 "4 Types of Organizational Culture," ArtsFWD, May 14, 2013, https://www.artsfwd.org/4-types-org-culture/.

43 Ibid.

44 "The History of Strategic Management," Harvard University, https://opentextbc.ca/strategicmanagement/chapter/the-history-of-strategic-management/.

45 Ibid.

46 Ibid.

47 "The Difference between Strategy and Tactics," Strategic Thinking Institute blog, May 1, 2014, https://www.strategyskills.com/ difference-strategy-tactics/.

48 Ibid.

49 "New Survey Shows Time's a Wastin'—Workers Goof Off More Than Two Hours a Day," American Management Association, April 8, 2019, https://www.amanet.org/articles/new-survey-shows-times-a-wastin-workers-goof-off-more-than-two-hours-a-day/.

50 "This Is How You Should Be Prioritizing Your Work and Life," Stephanie Vozza, *Fast Company*, April 9, 2018, https:// www.fastcompany.com/40552870/this-is-how-you-should-be-prioritizing-your-work-and-life.

51 "How to Write an Effective To-Do List," Divya Pahwa, PsychCentral, last updated July 8, 2018, https://psychcentral.com/blog/how-to-write-an-effective-to-do-list/.

52 Ibid.

53 "Are You Emotionally Intelligent? Here's How to Know for Sure," Travis Bradberry, PhD, TalentSmart, https://www.talentsmart.com/articles/Are-You-Emotionally-Intelligent--Here%E2%80%99s-How-to-Know-for-Sure-2102500910-p-1.html.

54 "This Is Why You Should Speak Up about Work Problems," Nicole Lyn Pesce, *MarketWatch*, July 12, 2018, https://www.marketwatch.com/story/this-is-why-you-should-speak-up-about-work-problems-2018-07-12.

55 Ibid.

56 "A New Study of 19 Million Meetings Reveals That Meetings Waste More Time Than Ever (but There Is a Solution)," Peter Economy, *Inc.*, January 11, 2019, https://www.inc.com/peter-economy/a-new-study-of-19000000-meetings-reveals-that-meetings-waste-more-time-than-ever-but-there-is-a-solution.html.

57 "9 Meeting Facilitation Skills for Managers" Dan McCarthy, The Balance Careers, updated June 3, 2019, https://www.thebalancecareers.com/meeting-facilitation-skills-2275915.

58 "Speaking Skills Top Employer Wish Lists. But Schools Don't Teach Them," Catherine Gewertz, *Education Week*, September 25, 2018, https://www.edweek.org/ew/articles/2018/09/26/speaking-skills-top-employer-wish-lists-but.html.

59 "If I Had More Time, I Would Have Written a Shorter Letter," Quote Investigator, https://quoteinvestigator.com/2012/04/28/shorter-letter/. Various versions of this quote have been attributed to Ernest Hemingway and others, but the true source appears to be Blaise Pascal.

60 "Why Your Meeting Needs Breaks," International Institute for Facilitation and Change , https://english.iifac.org/beatrice-briggs/why-your-meetings-need-breaks/.

61 According to Quote Investigator, this saying seems to have originated in 1908, in a short piece titled "Three Parts of a Sermon" published in the *Northern Daily Mail* of Durham, England. See https://quoteinvestigator.com/2017/08/15/tell-em/.

62 Prezi, "The 2018 State of Attention Report," https://prezi.com/resources/2018-state-of-attention-report/.

63 "Storytelling Best Practices to Increase Your Workplace Influence," Dana Brownlee, *Forbes*, November 16, 2019, https://www.forbes.com/sites/danabrownlee/2019/11/16/storytelling-best-practices-to-increase-your-workplace-influence/#1121bbb37b6c.

64 Ibid.

65 "Is Txting Ruining Ur Writing?!" *Scholastic News*, February 3, 2020, https://sn4.scholastic.com/issues/2019-20/020320/is-txting-ruining-ur-writing.html.

66 "Strategies for Communicating with All Five Generations in the Workforce," Walden Siew, *Employee Benefit News*, October 31, 2019, https://www.benefitnews.com/news/strategies-for-communicating-with-all-five-generations-in-the-workforce.

67 Ibid.

68 "Trust and Distrust in America," Lee Rainie, Scott Keeter, and Andrew Perrin, Pew Research Center, July 22, 2019, https://www.people-press.org/2019/07/22/trust-and-distrust-in-america/prc_2019-07-22_trust-distrust-in-america_0-01/.

69 Ibid.

70 "The State of Work–Life Balance in 2019: What We Learned from Studying 185 Million Hours of Working Time," Jory MacKay, RescueTime blog, January 24, 2019, https://blog.rescuetime.com/work-life-balance-study-2019/.

71 "The Results Are Clear: Long Hours Backfire for People and for Companies," Sarah Green Carmichael, *Harvard Business Review*, August 19, 2015, https://hbr.org/2015/08/the-research-is-clear-long-hours-backfire-for-people-and-for-companies.

72 This information appears in chapter 6 of my first book, *God Revealed: Revisit Your Past to Enrich Your Future* (New York: Morgan James Faith, 2013).

73 This assessment was created by Darren Shearer, founder of the Theology of Business Institute (www.TheologyofBusiness.com) and originally appeared in Darren's book, *The Marketplace Christian: A Practical Guide to Using Your Spiritual Gifts in Business.* © 2016 by Theology of Business. Reprinted with permission.